The power and poignancy of Desiree Ayres' story is loaded with uplifting hope and clear-eyed, practical help for people who have "been burned" by life circumstances. It's also a very useful, contemporary tool for striking the balance between "taking care of business" in your vocational career, and "building a full and healthy life." Here is a fascinating look at the life of a Hollywood "stunt-woman," who navigated disaster and now has become a solidly sensible wife, mother and pastor *"beyond the flame"* of pain and personal crisis. I commend the book: the writer offers workable insights for living, working and making a difference for good in today's fast-moving world—beginning with personally building a sane, sound and satisfying relationship with God and with the people in your life.

—Dr. Jack W. Hayford, Chancellor
The King's University, Los Angeles

Having known Desiree Ayres and her testimony that she has shared to countless thousands over the years, I can highly recommend that you read her book. Her miracle testimony builds the faith of the reader. Having been in the healing ministry, this book can play a major role in one's healing. God has healed Desiree and is using her to minister healing to others.

Beyond the Flame is a must read for anyone interested in gaining a practical and loving perspective of God's ultimate power and willingness to heal.

Oral Roberts

Beyond the Flame is a great book of God's love, mercy and loving kindness. Desiree is blessed to be alive and well (as I am) after a stunt went wrong and she was in an explosion.

I salute you and Mel and know Jesus is proud of you.

—Dodie Osteen
Co-Founder, Lakewood Church
Houston, Texas

Desiree Ayres is an amazing woman with a story that will move you and encourage you. In *Beyond the Flame* she shares her compelling story of surviving a fourteen-foot fire bomb while working as a stunt double. You will be inspired and enriched by Desiree's wisdom and remarkable story.

—Lisa Osteen Comes
Author, *You Are Made for More!*

Pastor Desiree Ayres is delightfully candid, encouraging, and completely engaging in her new book *Beyond the Flame*. You will get to know Pastor Desiree on a deeper and more personal level than ever before as she shares key moments in her life that transformed her forever. From the horrific accident that almost took her life to rediscovering God and love in a whole new way. This journey is worth reading.

—Dr. Don Colbert

Desiree Ayres provides a compelling account of her amazing story—the problems and pain, and how she encountered and embraced the promise of God! *Beyond the Flame* provides the reader with great hope, help, and encouragement as to what Jesus Christ can and will do in you and for you! Enjoy and be blessed!

—Keith Hershey
Missionary, Mutual Faith Missions

In this powerful book, *Beyond the Flame,* my friend Desiree Ayres shares, through her real life testimony, the power and grace of God. The story is intriguing, the principles are powerful, the Word is true, and the result is a miracle. Read it and expect the same!

—Dr. Dave Martin
America's #1 Christian Success Coach

The first time we met Desiree and Mel Ayres we were sitting at a restaurant having dinner. Harry and Mel were talking while Desiree and I were having our "girl to girl" talk. I gave her my testimony and then she began to tell me her story. Since being in the ministry for more than thirty years, I have heard many stories of tragedies and triumphs, but when Desiree started to unfold the details of her "walk through the fire," I was spellbound by every detail.

First of all, she is beautiful on the inside and equally gorgeous on the outside! I was looking at the most beautiful smiling face of what would become the dearest of all friends, and all of a sudden I realized that I must have missed a detail or two! She was talking about her face being burned in a firebomb while doing a stunt on one of her Hollywood stunt jobs. I stopped her and asked her to repeat what she had just said, because I mentally could not connect the dots of what she was saying! I mean, she's gorgeous, her face is beautiful, and it was burned in a fire?

OK, so you are going to have to read it for yourself. It's an amazing story with the most awesome miraculous outcome! Harry stopped Mel in mid-sentence as he had overheard what Desiree was saying to me as well. He asked, "Who are you talking about?" because outwardly he didn't think it could be her until he saw the pictures! We saw the pictures and we were amazed and still are at her testimony and we believe you will be, too! Only God can take the devastation that was meant to completely destroy her life, her appearance, her future, and her ministry, and turn it around so completely for His glory!

Desiree Ayres is a woman on fire for God! She has spent her adult life showing everyone who meets her how a person who has come through the flames of earthly fires can fulfill her destiny on this earth in the fire of almighty God! I have wanted her to write her life's story for many years and I thank God that it is ready! This book can touch you in a place inside the heart of God like no other. You will see for yourself as you read page after page what a life of obedience can do for you daily.

Desiree is a woman after God's own heart. She is a worshiper who has lost all her natural identity in the flames and fire of His presence, but not without much tragedy. King David said, "I will not give to God what cost me nothing."

Desiree Ayres is a woman who has given her life to God, and it cost her everything this world had to offer. Now she belongs to the King of kings forever. The natural fire Desiree has gone through would have made most people run from the call of God, but instead of running from Him, she has run to the fire of His presence shouting "Burn me up, Lord" to be an invisible worshiper for You!

As disfigured as Desiree was from the fire, she has come out, restored and glorified for the kingdom of God. Just as our Savior was disfigured, He came out for the whole world to see, not just Hollywood and what it had to offer. Desiree's life is a living testimony of how God can restore and bring glory to His name through adversity for the whole world to see.

—CHERYL SALEM
FORMER MISS AMERICA

Pastor Desiree Ayres is an amazing woman who has literally been through "the fire," and emerged to become a relentless force for God. Desiree is caring and tender, yet she possesses an unyielding strength in the things of God. This book is filled with faith in God's Word and a strong testimony of what God can do. Her message is clear…what God has done for her, He will certainly do for each one who will believe and call upon His name. You will be encouraged and strengthened as you journey with her through this horrible situation…to see how her faith in God turned tragedy into victory!

—DR. WENDY TREAT
CO-PASTOR, CHRISTIAN FAITH CENTER
SEATTLE, WASHINGTON

Bad things can happen to good people and, in a moment, our lives can be forever changed. For many, picking up the pieces and living life after a crisis can be more devastating than the crisis itself.

Desiree Ayres survived such an event and the life that she began living after has transformed her, her family, and the world she lives in. This book is a must read for all of us who want change, but don't know how and for those who want to move forward, but seem to slip back. Her insights, her honest and powerful life lessons, and her transparent heart reach out and show us that change is doable, dreams are possible, and one life can change our world.

—Pastor Deborah Cobrae
The Rock Church and
World Outreach Center

Beyond the Flame will inspire your faith to go above and beyond what you could ask or think. It gives you many examples of how to apply God's Word to your life to receive whatever you need to live and experience an overcoming, victorious life. It is an awesome testimony of her miraculous healing and her faith. You will be blessed, encouraged, and helped as you read.

—Apostle Frederick and Dr. Betty Price

CREATION HOUSE

Beyond the Flame

A Journey from Burning Devastation to Healing Restoration

DESIREE AYRES

Beyond the Flame—A Journey from Burning Devastation
to Healing Restoration
By Desiree Ayres
Published by Creation House
A Charisma Media Company
600 Rinehart Road
Lake Mary, Florida 32746
www.charismamedia.com

Design Director: Bill Johnson
Cover design by Nancy Panaccione
Photographs by Jim Jordan Photography

Visit the author's websites: www.ihpchurch.org and www.desireeayres.org.

Library of Congress Cataloging-in-Publication Data: 2012933339
International Standard Book Number: 978-1-61638-956-7
E-book International Standard Book Number: 978-1-61638-957-4

While the author has made every effort to provide accurate telephone numbers and Internet addresses at the time of publication, neither the publisher nor the author assumes any responsibility for errors or for changes that occur after publication.

First edition

12 13 14 15 16 — 9 8 7 6 5 4 3 2 1
Printed in the United States of America

DEDICATION

I dedicate this book:

To my amazing Lord and Savior Jesus Christ...

Thank You for healing me! Thank You for being my comfort in the midnight hour! Thank You for making a multitude of blessings out of the mess I got myself into. Thank You for taking away the pain! Thank You for doing exceedingly, abundantly, above all I can imagine, think, or hope for. Thank You for doing that for the person reading this book.

To my dad, Hubie Kerns...

Dad, thank you for praying for me for ten years until I met Jesus Christ. Thank you for not giving up on me. I look forward to seeing you again when I arrive in heaven. I could not write this book without thanking you for leading me into eternal life, and being there for me when I did not know if I would live or die. Thank you for your boldness, laughter, encouragement, and tender heart for our Lord and His people. Thank you for all the years of prayer and encouragement to preach the good news of the gospel of Jesus Christ. I love you, Dad!

To my husband, Mel Ayres…

How do I begin to thank the man who drew me to the Lord and inspired me to be an on-fire, sold-out bold Christian, to be a part of the greatest work on Planet Earth: populating heaven and plundering hell. Thank you for being the real deal, and the sacrifices you have made for the church, our friends, and our family. Thank you for being my knight in shining armor, and protecting me throughout these amazing thirty-plus years. Thank you for using your sword to fight the good fight of faith for and with me, and the amazing people God has brought into our lives. You are my best friend. You are the best friend any person could ever hope for. I admire, honor, and respect you as a husband, leader, anointed preacher, singer, songwriter, psalmist, pastor, and "my pastor." Thank you for being the greatest example of Jesus I have seen in human form. I love you, Mel Ayres!

ACKNOWLEDGMENTS

GLADYS DODD, WHAT would I do without you! What a gift from God you are. I would have never have made it to the point of being able to do this book without you. I would not be doing half the things I do without your faithful support all these years. Thank you for being the greatest servant and friend I could ever hope for.

Christine Rodela, what a treasure gift you are. Your peaceful, kind, gentle strength amazes me on a continual basis. Thank you for your love for the Lord, our church, and the call of God you see in me. Thank you for your prophetic words of encouragement at God's perfect timing.

Nikki Mata, you are a breath of fresh air and a joy to work with, with an attitude so filled with joy, it makes me smile being around you.

A special thank you to In His Presence women's team for your love, support, and believing in me and the ministry call on this book. I love you!

The wonderful generals in the body of Christ that did my forward and endorsements. You are my heroes!

Creation House team: Allen Quain and Robert Caggiano, thank you for answering my countless e-mails and talking with me giving me wisdom and calming advice during the process; and to Nancy Panaccione for her excellent cover design work.

Karen North, thank-you for your creative phrase,

heart, compassion, support and intercession during the process.

My church, In His Presence: I love you. What an honor to be your Pastor. You are the most fun, creative, sold-out on fire in love with Jesus people I have ever met. I love doing life with you. I love that I am not the only high drama person in the church!

CONTENTS

FOREWORD

AFTER READING *BEYOND the Flame*, all I could think was, "Well, that's the mother of all journeys right there—everything you need to know about God and life, all wrapped up in a heart-touching, gut-wrenching, thank-God-for-His-love-and-mercy, two-hour captivating read!"

For thirty years I've been married to this story and I have lived it every step of the way. Desiree Ayres' *Beyond the Flame* is her personal journey, yet despite that, her story will shape you. With the hottest branding iron heaven can produce, your soul will be fire-tattooed with edifying verbal jewels such as:

> "…if God would give you His only Son, what good thing will He withhold from you now?"

> "He's not mad at you, He's madly in love with you."

> "With God all things are possible, and without Him all things mean nothing at all."

That, like milk, will do a body good!

I know firsthand that *Beyond the Flame* happened just as it is written. I was there! When Desiree, as a successful young Hollywood stuntwoman surrounded by fame and fortune, found herself on fire with a passion to pursue Jesus Christ as her Lord and Savior, I was there. I was there when she found herself literally on fire in a tragic stunt accident and suffered second- and third-degree burns on her face, neck, and arms. And I was also there when the miraculous healing power and fire of the Holy Spirit "baffled" the best burn doctor in the nation and completely healed her in less than ten days.

I was there for each of these trials as I have been there these thirty years, yet as I was reading *Beyond the Flame* I was caught off guard. I wasn't expecting brand new tears. These were not the "Desiree, I wish it were me and not you!" tears I cried after her stunt accident. These were "Thank You, Jesus, it was You who took her burns and gave her Your skin and Your wholeness" tears of victory!

I love it when my thoughts, emotions, and my whole being are completely drenched in God's revealed understanding of His goodness and I am gushing with the best attempt at thanksgiving I can muster, repeating over and over again "Thank You, Jesus—thank You, Lord Jesus. Reading *Beyond the Flame* does that to you—and it does that for you.

I was also not anticipating a personal promise from the fourth Man who stood in the furnace as a shield and protector alongside Shadrach, Meshach, and Abednego. That same fourth Man also stood with Desiree, loving her, healing her, and restoring her with determination and power, as if He felt He had something to prove. His personal promise to me was…well, I'll let Him tell you, for He will be just as faithful and real to you, to promise you, to prophesy to you, and comfort you as you read and experience *Beyond the Flame*.

—MEL AYRES

PART ONE

INTRODUCTION

1

BORN IN HOLLYWOOD

I WAS BORN AT the Hollywood Presbyterian Hospital June 25…many years ago.

The first swim race I was ever in was for girls six years of age and under. My big sister was six; I was only four. She won the race, smiling ear to ear; I lost, crying and exhausted as I struggled to pull myself out of the Olympic-sized swimming pool. At one point during the race, I went to the side of the pool intending to give up and hang onto the edge, just so I could catch my breath and cry. That didn't work, however, because my dad came to the edge of the pool and shouted at the top of his lungs, "No! Swim! Go, go, go!" yelling and pointing the way to the other end of the pool.

My dad, along with all of the other swimmers who had finished the race, and their families, started cheering for me to keep swimming. As I gaspingly made it to the end of the pool, I came up out of the water and stood on the deck, dramatically crying, I have to admit, I did feel better as the audience applauded me for finishing the race. I was especially happy when they gave me a ribbon and took a picture of me with the rest of the racers.

Little did I know then, at four years old, I was already

being groomed for my future as one of Hollywood's top water stuntwomen.

My older brother, sister and I all trained at the Woodland Hills Swim School. Swim meets and races were part of our growing-up years. I loved to swim and always gave it my all. And I loved the trophies.

When I was twelve, one of our assignments was to swim as fast as we could for twenty-five yards without taking a breath. This part was a piece of cake for me. As soon as we finished, we had only a few seconds to catch our breath before we were to do it all over again. On my second lap I would slip in two or three breaths, but the coach caught me and put me on the side aisle so he could watch me more closely. Now every time I slipped in a breath, he whacked me on the head with a kick-board. I'd leave practices with terrible headaches. One day I told my mom that I no longer wanted to become a professional swimmer, and I pulled out of my daily practices.

I still loved to swim, and enjoyed our pool, summers at the beach riding waves, surfing, water skiing, and every water sport imaginable. In high school I started to compete in swim races again. Now workouts were much easier and I enjoyed being on a relay team that made it to the championship games and won. I also swam in two-mile ocean swims while living in Manhattan Beach, ran 10k races, and went on to run a marathon.

When I was sixteen, I went with my mom to pick up my sister one day from her swim workout. On that particular day a crew was there interviewing swimmers for a Lady Schick hair dryer commercial. The assistant director looked over at me and asked if I would read a line from the script. I did that for the director and landed my very first job in the motion picture industry. I was ecstatic! On that commercial alone I made thousands of dollars! Making this kind of money at so young an age made an impression on me, and the prospect of earning that much again eventually led me into pursuing a full-time career in the industry.

I finished high school and went on to college. During my summer breaks I would work as an extra in films. Barely noticed and definitely on the bottom of the totem pole as far as movie directors, producers, and others in the industry are concerned. Extras are the people you see in the background of a film scene walking, dancing, or perhaps sitting in a stadium, and so forth. One day on the set I watched a stuntwoman in a fight being pushed into a swimming pool. I later learned that she made six hundred dollars for the stunt, while I just made sixty dollars as an extra. "Push me into the pool," I thought. "I can do that, especially with my background in swimming, and my family connections."

Being in the stunt business ran in my family. My dad, Hubie Kerns, was the stuntman for Adam West as well as the stunt coordinator on the original Batman television series. At that time he was the highest-paid stuntman in the business. He held the worlds record for the 4:40 race, and the two times he qualified for the Olympics he was not able to compete, because the Olympics had been canceled due to World War II. My dad faithfully served our country during the war, and missed his dream of winning the gold medal. He attended the University of Southern California where he was not only a track star, but also played football. Once the ball was passed to him, no one could catch him! The director of the famous movie, Jim Thorpe—All-American cast my dad in a lead role playing opposite Burt Lancaster.

My mom, Dorismae Kerns, was a publicity writer at MGM studios and became close friends with Elizabeth Taylor, who is my brother's godmother. My brother became a stuntman (and still is today), and so I naturally followed them into the motion picture industry.

I started to train at a stunt school and later landed my first job doubling for Lynda Day George and Stella Stevens, both in one day! I was flown over to Catalina Island where I was a scuba diver for Linda's scene. Then I changed my wig and costume and swam in the ocean for Stella's scene. I found myself making over six hundred dollars a day. I remember thinking, "Wow, I've found my career!"

Water work was always easy for me, so it was like I was getting paid to play. However, to work more consistently in the business, I had to learn other stunts, like high falls, car crashes, fire burns, fight scenes, and so on.

When I landed the stunt job of doubling for Daisy Duke on the television series Dukes of Hazzard, my career skyrocketed. I was doing acting parts in commercials and on various shows, including The Incredible Hulk, 240-Robert, and the film Brainstorm.

Even though my career was taking off and I appeared to be happy and successful, I felt empty on the inside. Something was missing.

THE MISSING PIECE

I met my future husband in an acting class in Burbank, California. When I first saw Mel Ayres, I flipped over him. I started to have dreams about him, and in the

4

dreams we were in love and living happily ever after. During class I'd try to get Mel's attention. I'd wear low-cut leopard outfits, tight short skirts, and short shorts. Nothing seemed to work. I later learned that Mel was a strong Christian, and two years before I'd met him he had made a commitment to be celibate. So the harder I tried to get his attention, the more he kept his distance.

This rejection left me frustrated and hurt. I was already battling anorexia and bulimia, to a point where my hair was starting to fall out and my fingernails were starting to fall off. Yet, amazingly enough, at the same time I was living in Manhattan Beach and winning bikini contests. I looked healthy on the outside, but I was dying on the inside.

About six months after I met Mel, I found out that my cousin Michael had become a born-again Christian. One day Michael invited me to attend church with him. As soon as he said the word church, I thought about Mel.

"What kind of a church?" I asked.

He said, "A Christian church."

"Right answer," I thought, as my heart leaped at the thought of running into Mel. Maybe I could finally talk with him, and once he got to know me, I was sure he'd fall in love with me.

"Where's the church located?" I asked.

Michael answered, "Westwood."

"Bingo," I thought. "Second right answer." I knew that Mel, the good Christian boy who always carried his Bible, lived in Westwood.

"Yes!" I immediately responded. "I would love to go to church with you this Sunday."

Man of My Dreams

Boy, was I in for a surprise. I had never been in a Spirit-filled church before where you could feel the tangible presence of God. During the music and singing I began to cry and didn't even know why. At one point I looked up at the front row and saw Mel, the man of my dreams, with his hands raised in the air. I thought, "Why are his hands in the air? Have I fallen in love with some kind of monk or something?"

But as I looked around, I saw that almost everyone had their hands in the air. Now this really rocked my world. I was sure that I had experienced every kind of spiritual practice there was. My mom was a New Age psychic while I was growing up, my dad was a Christian Scientist, and my best friend was a Mormon. I had jumped with Hare Krishnas, chanted with New Agers, astral-projected, and attended churches of nearly every denomination. You name it. I thought I had tried it all, until this day, that is, when I found myself crying because of the awesome presence of God that I was sensing. The preacher shared a sermon and talked about how to receive Jesus Christ as Lord and Savior. I went home that day and invited the Lord into my heart.

Within six weeks from the day I asked Jesus into my heart, I became born again, baptized in the Holy Spirit, and married to the man of my dreams!

Our second date was pretty funny. You see, my dad became a born-again Christian ten years before I did, and he prayed for me and tried so hard to get me to know this amazing Jesus. I thought he was crazy and had become a religious nut, a "Jesus freak." How wrong, naive, and judgmental I was! I see that now that my spiritual eyes are open to the truth. Our second date was to Crenshaw Christian Center. My dad was overjoyed to hear I had a date with a Christian and was going to hear Dr. Price, whom he loved. He called me that morning to see if Mel had picked me up yet. I told him that Mel had called and his car had broken down, so the date was canceled. My dad said, "Give me his number." I did, and he called him and picked Mel up in Westwood. Then he picked me up in Manhattan Beach, and took us to church to make sure this date happened. It was that day that I experienced the power of the Holy Spirit as well as a love for the Word of God that would change my life forever!

After our whirlwind marriage in Las Vegas, Mel and I returned to Southern California where we loved growing in the things of God together. Within six months Jesus healed me of anorexia and bulimia. I've written my testimony about this healing in my book titled God Hunger.[1] I was so thankful to God for all He had done in my life to that point, that I led people to the Lord almost every day I worked on a movie set. Before my conversion I used to be excited about what show I was working on or who I was going to double for. Now I was excited about who received Jesus as their Savior, who got baptized in the Holy Spirit, who got healed when I prayed for them, or whom I had the opportunity to share the good news of the gospel with.

Mel and I loved God, we loved each other, and we loved people. We were always ministering to others, and we loved every minute of it. Still do, to this day!

SPIRITUAL TUG OF WAR

Everything seemed to be going fine in our lives. But then something changed. It was when Mel and I were working together on the soap opera *Days of Our Lives*, Mel as an actor, and I as the stunt coordinator. On the set Mel talked and ministered to one of the security guards who at one time had been a pastor of a church but now was heartbroken. When the director would call for Mel, he'd get frustrated, because he found that he'd rather be ministering to the security guard than acting.

When we got home from work one night, Mel said, "Desiree, don't pay my Screen Actors Guild dues anymore. I'm out."

"What!" I said in disbelief. "We've worked so hard to get where we are. You're a working actor, and now you want out?"

"Yes," he replied, and I knew that I was not going to change his mind. I also knew I needed to support my husband in the desires of his heart and be an encouragement to him.

Mel continued to wait tables, and he worked his heart out at our local church. "That's fine for him," I remember thinking, "but I like my career." I enjoyed the amount of money I made every week. My thought was that someone needs to pay the bills.

But I began to feel a tug-of-war going on inside of me. Here we'd be in church listening to special guest speakers, and my beeper would go off. So I'd leave to go on an interview or to work while my husband sat under the anointed Word of God with our friends. I felt like God had something for me to catch in the spirit realm, and He wanted me there in church, but it seemed like I couldn't resist putting the industry first in my life. I was taught growing up to have strong work ethics, to be on time, and to do whatever it takes to make it to the top. And I had that money hook in my jaw, along with the drive for success.

SENSING DANGER

One day I was working on a Coca-Cola commercial when I became grieved in my spirit. Even though I was a relatively young Christian, I believed that God was letting me know in my knower that something was wrong. I called my husband and a couple of strong Christian friends and asked them to pray for me while I worked that day. My job was to ride as a passenger in a tiny plane that was doing tricks of every kind. We'd do circle after circle in the air. At the end of the day the pilot was to fly the plane low and take off the top of some trees (already precut to split apart easily).

I knew in my spirit that this was the danger zone. We did the shot, while I prayed quietly the whole time. "Perfect!" shouted the director, as the entire cast and crew applauded our magnificent stunt. Then the director said, "One more time," and I knew this next film shot was the reason I had been grieved all day; the grieving became worse as we climbed into the plane for what would be the shot of the day, barely escaping death.

Once again the plane swooped down to take off the top of the trees, but this time we came in too close, which caused the plane to wobble and the pilot to head us straight up into the air. As we headed upward, the plane engine died. The pilot nervously began to signal that we were in trouble. Fire engines already on hand because of the potential danger of this stunt, came racing into view as we were now headed straight down to the ground. Immediately I cried out to Jesus to save us and began praying in tongues—loudly!

Somehow I knew that now my own words would not be enough in this situation and that I had to pray the perfect prayer for divine intervention. Just before our crash unto death, the engine started up. Needless to say, everyone on the set that day was shaken up, but no one had knees shaking as badly as the pilot and I as we stepped out of the plane.

Now this stunt pilot was known as the best in the business. But several weeks later he died in a stunt plane accident. I honestly believe that we would have both died that day on the set had I not sought divine intervention and prayed in the Holy Ghost for God's supernatural power to show up on the scene. God in His faithfulness saved my life from an early death.

When I got home that night and told Mel what had happened, he simply asked, "Desiree, why don't you just get out?" I was stunned. "And do what?" I replied. "Work in a grocery store [something I had done while I was in high school]? Go back to having tough financial times? I don't think so." I could not see doing anything but what I had strived so hard to be good at.

At that time I was considered Hollywood's number one water stuntwoman. I was getting even more acting work on shows like *The Incredible Hulk*, *Matt Houston*, *Riptide*, *T. J. Hooker*, *Police Story*, and *Miami Vice*. By now I was doing stunts for Loni Anderson, Heather Thomas on *The Fall Guy*, Ann Jillian, Emma Samms, and dozens of other actresses. It had taken me years to get to this place, I justified in my mind. And now I'm to give it all up? I couldn't imagine doing so—and did not want to.

There it was, that money hook in my jaw, at a time when I was feeling a spiritual tug-of-war. Money, position, and fame kept me in a career even though I believed that God wanted to move me forward into the higher calling He had, just for me.

Learning the Hard Way

It would have been so much easier to have learned my lesson simply by hearing God and then obeying the Holy Spirit's guidance and the wise counsel of my husband.

Have you found that you too have had to learn lessons the hard way? I sure did—you'll see in chapter two, where I describe a horrific accident that changed my life forever. That lesson grew me up quickly and I now make decisions daily to spend time in the Word and in prayer. First thing in the morning I sit at the feet of Jesus and learn my life lessons the easy way—the pain-free way.

The Bible says in Exodus 20:3 that we are to have no other gods before Him. In Deuteronomy 6:14 it says, "You shall not go after other gods." This includes the god of money. I was making my decision to stay in the industry based on money. Well, let me tell you, no amount of money is worth having your face burnt up and your life nearly snuffed out.

I pray that as you read my story you'll choose to learn your life lessons the easy way, sitting at the feet of Jesus and listening to the guidance of His Holy Spirit.

2

THE ACCIDENT THAT
CHANGED MY LIFE

LEADING UP TO the stunt accident that changed everything for me, life was good. While my career continued to flourish, I began to notice the different atmospheres among the productions I worked on. For example, some felt alive and happy; others felt dark and gloomy. One show in particular felt very dark, and I didn't like working there. I knew there was a lot of drug use going on around the set, and because of that, mistakes were all too common.

In fact, a few other stunt people had been burned, and one young stuntman had been killed a few short months before my dreadful day on the set.

I was called to work on this particular television series for one week, doubling for a guest-starring actress. Everything went fine even though all week long I sensed an evil presence on the set. While I couldn't put my finger on just what it was, I did feel that God was displeased that I had taken this job.

The following week, I worked over at Warner Brothers Studio with a Christian stunt coordinator, doubling for an actress swimming in a lagoon. In this stunt I was being chased by an alligator. Now this was my kind of stunt, especially since the alligator was a mechanical one! I was only on the show for a day when I received a telephone call to come back to my previous assignment, for one more day for another shot they needed to do.

My stunt was to be a passenger in a 4x4 truck driving down a dusty road on a desert terrain. As the driver drove the vehicle, at a certain point I was to press a button rigged to make the hood of the vehicle go up in smoke. I was then to jump out of the vehicle and roll along the hard dirt ground. I remember feeling a knot in my stomach and a strong sense that the Holy Spirit did not want me to go. But what came out of my mouth was, "Sure, I'll be there!" There it was again, that money hook in my jaw that made me want to work every day and as much as I could.

Little did I realize then that this would be the last day that money would have a stronghold in my life or lead and guide me to any decision I would make in the future.

"Please, Pray for Me"

When I arrived on the set early on the morning of February 25, 1985, I was grieved in every part of my being—so much so that I called strong Christians I knew, including my husband, and asked them to pray for me. I prayed all morning, but I couldn't shake the grieving inside of me.

My stunt bag consisted of special shoes, along with knee, elbow, and hip pads, and other gear, depending on what the job was. At the last minute I decided to throw on a pair of gloves, which, thankfully, ended up keeping my hands from being burned. I also had on a wig that protected my hair and scalp.

When the director called for our stunt, the stuntman began to drive. At the designated spot, I hit the button that was to make the hood of the vehicle go up in smoke, and then I dove out of the truck. That was the last thing I remembered for quite some time. I was not aware then that I had dived into a fourteen-pound fire bomb and been knocked out completely.

When I finally came to, I could hear voices all around me. I heard a fireman talking, the first AD (assistant director) asking me questions and other stunt people standing around talking. I knew something had gone terribly wrong; I just didn't know how bad it really was. At that point I had to wonder just how close to death I was or if I had any arms or legs.

In addition I felt this dark, evil presence surrounding me, one of death and destruction. I felt like Satan himself was trying to kill me. I opened my mouth and began to pray in the Spirit, calling out to God, my Creator, my Healer, my Savior, the One who truly could help me out of this horrible mess I was in. I could hear the director yelling in the background to get me out of the way because they were already setting up to shoot the next scene. While most of the crew had moved to the next shot, I lay on the ground, struggling to breathe and literally fighting for my life.

I'd heard it said on film sets, "Time is money." And since the producers and directors were paying a lot of people a lot of money to work that day, they didn't want actors wasting their time watching to see if Desiree the stuntwoman would live or die. Believe me, this whole experience was a real eye-opener.

HEART-TO-HEART WITH GOD

Trying to help me understand what was going on around me, the assistant director told me that a helicopter was on its way to pick me up and take me to the Sherman Oaks Burn Center. He told me that I had been burned, and he asked me who I'd like for him to call. I said, "Please call my husband. He needs to start praying for me," and I told him the phone number. He asked if there was anyone else. I said, "Yes, please call my dad for me too." I also gave him the number of one of my best friends.

While I was lying on the ground, firemen were pouring a cool water solution on my face. They asked me if I could feel anything. I told them that I couldn't. My body was still in major shock. During my helicopter ride parts of my face began to feel like they were on fire. The fireman continued to pour the solution on me to help ease the pain.

On that ride I had a serious heart-to-heart talk with God. For the first time I saw how foolish it was to be so consumed with money. The love of money, which the Bible says is the root of all kinds of evil (1 Tim. 6:10), had taken me down a dark path. Oh, what I would have given to have made a different decision that day when I was called upon to do this stunt. Right then, I told God that my successful career was over and that I would never again do another stunt.

I told God that whatever He wanted me to do and however He could use me, I wanted to live my life completely for Him. I needed Him so badly right then. He had always been so good to me, and here I had disobeyed Him and found myself in a terrible mess. But I knew about God's unconditional love. I knew that, no matter what, He was still my Father, my Creator, my Healer, the One I could turn to in my time of need. In the helicopter that day I was crying out to Him in every part of my being. "Oh, God, please help me!"

I believed then—and still do—that when we turn to Him in our afflictions, He can make a multitude of blessings out of any mess we have gotten ourselves into. He certainly did for me, and I know He will do it for you, because His Word in Acts 10:34 says that God shows no partiality. That means that He is not a respecter of persons. What He does for one, He will do for another. Maybe not always in the same way, but He will help each one of us in our times of need.

CRITICAL CONDITION

When the helicopter landed at the hospital, everything was a bit of a blur. Doctors and nurses quickly moved around me. My burnt clothes were cut off. The medical staff was talking doctor talk, and someone was shooting me full of morphine. I was admitted into the intensive care unit and listed in critical condition with second- and third-degree burns on my entire face, neck, chest, arms, and wrists.

I had inhaled fumes, which were affecting my lungs, and was also having an allergic reaction to the morphine, so I began throwing up. Eventually I had to tell medical personnel to stop all medications, which meant that I would go through this entire ordeal without painkillers.

By the time my husband arrived at the burn center, my head was wrapped in white bandages and holes were cut out for my eyes, nose, and mouth. I'm sure I must have looked like a mummy. Mel took one look at me and broke into tears. He could see that my upper lip was burnt off and that I was fighting for my life.

Here I had been waiting for my husband, my spiritual rock, to show up. Mel was and still is strong in Christ, a mighty man of faith, so when I saw him break into tears at the sight of me, I knew I was in real trouble. I had never seen my husband this broken. Soon after, my dad came into my hospital room. He broke into uncontrollable sobbing. This didn't bother me as much as seeing Mel weep, because I remember as a young girl seeing my dad, so tenderhearted, crying as we watched episodes of Lassie.

Shortly after that my best friend walked in, and she broke into tears. I realized then that I was a real mess and a prime candidate for a miracle.

By now my vomiting had turned into dry heaves, so I again asked to be taken off of all pain medication. I decided I would trust God completely in every area of my ordeal. I knew that He was able to help me. Thankfully I had the support of some strong people of God.

That night my accident was on the news, so word was out. Christian brothers and sisters from our church called Trinity Broadcasting Network, Christian Broadcasting Network, and other prayer circles. People all over the country—and the world—were praying for me. And, believe me, not only could I feel the prayers of the saints, but I was ready to watch God show up and show off.

The next several days should have been the worst of my life. But in the midst of pain my miracle began to happen. I would end up leaving the Sherman Oaks Burn

Center a mere ten days later completely healed. Glory to God!

I believe God showed me some key insights on receiving my miracle during my hospital stay, and I'd like to share them with you. I believe if you will apply these principles to your life, you too can receive your miracle. Mine was one of physical healing. You may need healing in relationships or in your finances. I believe these insights will work for you just as they did for me. I pray the words of this book will minister life, hope, and encouragement to you and that you will know God has a miracle for you!

PART TWO

MY TEN-DAY
MIRACLE

3

IN A CRISIS, CALL OUT
TO YOUR CREATOR

N O MATTER HOW challenging or difficult your present circumstance may be, I can assure you of one thing: As you cry out to God in your crisis, He can and will bring you help. Not only will He help you, but He can also make a multitude of blessings out of any situation. Be encouraged, because as you cry out to your Creator, He can and will turn your mess into a message, your test into a testimony!

In my case it was a mess that could have easily been avoided. I felt the Holy Spirit leading me not to take that particular job that day. I knew better. But the minimum amount of five hundred dollars I'd make for just showing up that day, plus my pay adjustment depending on the stunt I was doing, was just too attractive. I tried to rationalize away the leading of the Lord, which was a huge mistake that had left many of us crying out to God for help. That day after my accident, I saw clearly that money means nothing to a person facing the possibility of having their face scarred for the rest of their life or worse, not even knowing if you will live and make it through the day.

As I stated in the previous chapter, when I finally regained consciousness after the explosion, I knew something was terribly wrong, and I felt this dark evil presence around me. I know now that death and destruction were trying to take my life. When I awoke, it was a very dark eerie feeling to not feel my body, not knowing if body parts were missing or how bad the damage was. I did know that I'd been hurt badly. Everything was so blurry with the yelling and shouting and as paramedics on the set were running over to me. Stunt people and others were getting as close as they could to see what had happened.

I believe the devil tried to kill me that day, but his attack failed. Why? I believe a big key is that I cried out to God, and He intervened on my behalf.

I cried out to Him, knowing He would hear me and care for me. I remembered what the Bible says: "Lord, I cry out to You; make haste to me! Give ear to my voice when I cry out to You" (Ps. 141:1).

Psalm 50:15 says, "Call upon Me in the day of trouble; I will deliver you, and you shall glorify Me." What a wonderful promise that is!

God tells us to call on Him when we're in trouble and He will deliver us. "And you shall glorify Me," the verse concludes. In other words, once He delivers you, you can testify of the goodness of God and of what He's done for you, and how He got you out of your mess and turned it into a message.

Here are additional scriptures that should encourage you even more to call out to God in your time of need:

> Trust in, lean on, rely on, and have confidence in
> Him at all times, you people; pour out your hearts

before Him. God is a refuge for us (a fortress and a high tower). Selah [pause, and calmly think of that]!
—PSALM 62:8, AMP

Then they cry out to the Lord in their trouble, and He brings them out of their distresses.
—PSALM 107:28

Have you ever been distressed? This says that if you cry out to the Lord in your trouble, He will bring you out of your sorrow, pain, and distressful situation.

Then you shall call, and the Lord will answer; you shall cry, and He will say, "Here I am."
—ISAIAH 58:9

It doesn't matter how many times the storms of life knock you down. You can rise up after each fall, because God in heaven is there for you. That's good news!
Psalm 57:1–3 says:

Be merciful to me, O God, be merciful to me! For my soul trusts in You; and in the shadow of Your wings I will make my refuge, until these calamities have passed by. I will cry out to God Most High, to God who performs all things for me. He shall send from heaven and save me; He reproaches the one who would swallow me up.

This says that God will take care of the things in life that concern you. He'll send angels from heaven to save you. And He'll reproach the devil on your behalf.

When you call out to God in times of crisis and when you press into Him, He shows up and gives you the faith you need to climb whatever mountain you may be facing.

I had only been a Christian for two years at the time of my accident, but I was a fireball for Christ. I spent time daily getting to know Him and being in His Word, the Bible. Because of that I knew the importance of calling out to God in my time of need.

We're all being called to know God and to press into Him more. No matter how long you've been a Christian, how much revelation you've had, or how many miracles you've experienced, you can always get to know Him better. Do you know how vast God is? We serve a big God, a huge and glorious God. The Bible tells us that there are creatures in heaven circling Him saying, "Holy, holy, holy," because every time they go around Him, they get a new glimpse of His glory.

There are so many supernatural and glorious experiences we're supposed to be having with Him here on Planet Earth on a regular basis. He wants us to get a glimpse of His glory too. But to do that we need to spend time with Him and get to know Him more. Here are five power points to help you do just that.

1. Daily practice pressing into God

In times of trouble we need to automatically cry out to God and press in for His help and for His answers. But to do that we need to daily make a decision to press in. Why? We have so many things in our lives to distract us: kids, spouses, jobs, cell phones, text messaging, computers, e-mails, Facebook, Twitter, MySpace, blogging…and the list goes on and on, to daily pull us in a hundred different directions.

Wouldn't it be great to be able to check into a hotel for

a few days where we wouldn't have anything else to do but pray, fast, and just hear from heaven? Well, most of us can't do that on a regular basis, but we can make an effort every day to spend time in God's Word to learn about Him and to hear what He has to say, especially if we are in distress. I love what He says in Psalm 107:28. We referred to it earlier, but it bears repeating: "Then they cry out to the Lord in their trouble, and He brings them out of their distresses."

My crisis was finding myself lying on the ground after flying out of a burning vehicle and ending up in the Sherman Oaks Burn Center with second- and third-degree burns on my face, neck, chest, arms, and wrists. What's distressing you today?

- Do you have more bills than money to pay them?

- Did you total your car in a traffic accident?

- Is your body racked with pain?

- Are you hurt because someone has broken your heart?

- Has someone you love died?

- Are you filled with so much discouragement that you can't see straight?

- Has someone told you that you're worthless?

These are just a few of the trials that face people every day. What is it that may be causing you pain and sorrow? Whatever it is, cry out to the Lord in your trouble, and He will answer you and bring you out of it. Remember

Isaiah 58:9: "Then you shall call, and the LORD will answer. You shall cry, and He will say, 'Here I am.'"

Here's a bonus. Hebrews 11:6 says that God is a rewarder of those who diligently seek Him. So not only will He bring us out of our distresses, but He'll reward us as well. How?

Are you a parent? Have you ever used the reward system to teach your children? We reward our children for good behavior, right? Do you think God, our Father, might do the same? So if we enjoy rewarding our children, how much more does God enjoy rewarding us when we diligently seek Him?

Because I had practiced seeking God prior to my accident and was learning from His Word daily, I had already experienced His power to help me in other situations; so when it happened, I knew automatically to cry out to Him.

2. Trust completely in God

We're going to discuss the issue of putting our complete heart trust in God more in chapter 5, so we won't go into detail here. But in pressing into God during our times of crisis, we need to trust that He's going to make everything OK. That He's going to do what His Word says He'll do and deliver us from our distresses. That He's going to give us the answers we need to live correctly, even if those answers don't always make sense.

Proverbs 3:5–6 tells us: "Trust in the Lord with all your heart, and lean not on your own understanding. In all your ways acknowledge Him, and He shall direct your paths."

Remember the passage from Psalm 62:8, where it says that God is a refuge for us? I'm so glad to know He is my safe haven, my place of sanctuary, and that I have a place to go in my time of need. So do you.

3. Remember, trials don't last forever

Isn't it great to know that our trials don't last forever? Look at what 1 Peter 1:3–6 says:

> Blessed be the God and father of our Lord Jesus Christ, who according to His abundant mercy has begotten us again to a living hope through the resurrection of Jesus Christ from the dead, to an inheritance incorruptible and undefiled and that does not fade away, reserved in heaven for you, who are kept by the power of God through faith for salvation ready to be revealed in the last time. In this you greatly rejoice, though now *for a little while*, if need be, you have been grieved by various trials.
>
> —EMPHASIS ADDED

This verse doesn't say that you're going to be grieved by the same trials year after year after year, for the rest of your life. It says "for a little while." Trials pass. They blow over. When you're in the midst of one, it's good to remind yourself that it's only for a little while, and this too will pass.

It's like a woman giving birth to a baby. Throughout the process she often experiences lots of pain, even agony, and it's not unusual for her to scream out. Now, some women have pain-free deliveries, and praise God for them, but most women go through considerable pain while giving birth. And when they're in the middle of it, they think, "I'm never going to do this again." But then time goes by, and they decide they want to have another baby. Why? Because their experience was grievous, but just for a little while. Their pain didn't last forever.

First Peter 1:7 goes on to say, "That the genuineness of your faith, being much more precious than gold that perishes, though it is tested by fire, may be found to praise, honor and glory at the revelation of Jesus Christ." Often when we're grieved by trials, it causes us to press into God more and to walk by faith. Pressing into the Lord will give you a glimpse into the spirit realm and into what God says about your situation. Your faith then allows you to believe what you're seeing in the spirit realm more than what you're seeing in the natural. Now that's what it means to walk by faith.

Verses 8–11 say, "Whom having not seen you love. Though now you do not see Him, yet believing, you rejoice with joy inexpressible and full of glory, receiving the end of your faith—the salvation of your souls. Of this salvation the prophets have inquired and searched carefully, who prophesied of the grace that would come to you, searching what, or what manner of time, the Spirit of Christ who was in them was indicating when He testified beforehand the sufferings of Christ and the glories that would follow."

So sometimes when you're going through a suffering experience, you need to remember that there's a glory that follows. In my case, while in the hospital, I suffered terribly with physical pain. As I would press into God and His glory would fill me, not only was my body pain free, but also my whole spirit, soul, and body were filled with the ecstasy of the glory of God. The glory that follows is that not only did God give me a miracle, but also He now uses me to minister His healing power to others. I get to be a vessel that experiences the glory of God pouring through me to others.

The tangible healing anointing is a glorious thing to experience. I've had the privilege of laying hands on thousands of people who have been healed by Jesus. Weekly I have the honor of praying for people in the church that Mel and I co-pastor here in Southern California and to experience His glorious healing presence on a regular basis.

4. Have no other gods before Him

Having no other gods before God is so key to not getting sidetracked in our Christian walk. In fact, we are warned in Scripture to keep ourselves from idols and not to allow anything to take first place in our hearts except Jesus. First John 5:21 says, "Little children, keep yourselves from idols (false gods)—[from anything and everything that would occupy the place in your heart due to God, from any sort of substitute for Him that would take first place in your life]" (AMP).

Remember, the devil loves to trip us up by getting us to love something or someone more than we love God. It might be your job, your home, your ministry, your idea of what success really is, maybe even your family members. But listen; in your times of crisis, no matter how much you cry out to all these things, they will never be able to deliver you out of your troubles like Jesus can. Don't be deceived. Cry out to God in your time of need. He's the only One who can deliver you.

Don't let the enemy trap you into going down a road you were never called to go down. Keep God first place in your life, and He will protect you. God will never lead you down a path to cause destruction and harm to purposely come your way. But if you love something more than you love God, you'll pay more attention to that voice, which could very well lead you to a place where the enemy would love to snuff out your life. And wipe out your life, he will try, because the devil comes to rob, kill, steal, and destroy. (See John 10:10.) The devil tried to kill me that day on the Hollywood set, but I cried out to my heavenly Father, and God delivered me out of my distress. I thank God for the rest of John 10:10, where Jesus tells us He came that we might have life and have it more abundantly. I am praying that your days are filled with the abundant life Jesus has for you and that you have His wisdom and strength to obey His voice and not fall prey to follow the voice of the deceiver.

5. Continue to walk in love

God made you and me to be love vessels and to walk in love. So another ploy the enemy uses to sabotage a Christian's call, blessings, destiny, and meaningful times of pressing into the Lord is to get you to be hateful and unforgiving. Have you noticed that life is full of opportunities to love and forgive others? God is the perfect example of love, and since we are created in His image, we are called to love.

First Peter 1:22 says, "Since you have purified your souls in obeying the truth through the Spirit in sincere love of the brethren, love one another fervently with a pure heart."

First Peter 4:8 tells us, "And above all things have fervent love for one another, for 'love will cover a multitude of sins.'"

God invites you to cry out to Him in your times of trouble. Do so, knowing that He will answer when you call, deliver you from your distresses, and send angels, if need be, to save you. (See Matthew 13:41–43.)

Do you need to know God more so that you can automatically call out to Him in your time of need? Remember these five power points to help you know God:

1. Daily practice pressing into God.

2. Trust completely in God.

3. Remember, trials don't last forever.

4. Have no other gods before Him.

5. Continue to walk in love.

The following is a great example of someone who called out to his father in his time of need:

> While kayaking in southern England off the Isle of Wight, Mark Ashton-Smith, a thirty-three-year-old lecturer at Cambridge University, capsized in treacherous waters. Clinging to his craft and reaching for his cell phone, Ashton-Smith's first inclination was to call his father. It didn't matter to the desperate son that his dad, Alan Pimm-Smith, was at work training British troops in Dubai thirty-five hundred miles away. Without delay the father relayed his son's Mayday to the Coast Guard installation nearest to his son's location. Ironically it was less than a mile away. Within twelve minutes a helicopter rescued the grateful Ashton-Smith.[1]

Like this kayaker, when we are in a crisis, our first impulse should be to call on our Father—our heavenly

Father. "Call upon Me in the day of trouble; I will deliver you" (Ps. 50:15).

God created us; therefore He knows every cell in our bodies and the number of hairs we have on our heads. Psalm 139 talks about how God formed us in our mothers' wombs and how He is familiar with all of our ways.

He created us and is acquainted with all our ways; no one knows better than God how to heal our bodies, repair our relationships, and fix the things in our lives that concern us. Since He knows best, we need to remember to call out to our Creator in our times of trouble.

4

PRAY IN THE HOLY SPIRIT

WHEN I DOVE out of that burning truck on the day of my accident and finally came to, the first thing I did was cry out to God. I just cried, "Oh, God." Then, almost immediately, I began praying in tongues. I didn't know the full extent of what had gone wrong, but I did know that this was a crisis situation for me. I knew right then that I needed my heavenly Father to intervene for me. As I said earlier, I didn't know what had happened. I didn't know if I had arms or legs, but I could feel the spirit of death all over me. The devil tried his best to kill me that day, but he was unsuccessful.

And you know, as I was praying in the Holy Spirit, I didn't care what anyone thought. Right at that moment it was just me and God. I didn't even know if I was dead. I didn't know if I was going to die by the end of the day. I just knew that I had to connect with my heavenly Father, and it didn't matter what anyone else thought of me.

I knew at that moment that if I would cry out and pray in tongues, I would be praying the perfect prayer. I knew that the Holy Spirit would make intercession for me and that He'd have a heavenly host of ministering angels come on the scene for me. I knew that my God would do whatever it took to meet my need. All I had to do was use my gift of praying in tongues.

Praying in this manner is such a powerful gift that's available to all believers. It's what makes you a powerhouse for God. It's a gift that will help you in your time of trouble. Here's what Romans 8:26–27 has to say about praying in the Holy Ghost:

> Likewise the Spirit also helps in our weaknesses. For we do not know what we should pray for as we ought, but the Spirit Himself makes intercession for us with groanings which cannot be uttered. Now He who searches the hearts knows what the mind of the Spirit is, because He makes intercession for the saints according to the will of God.

The power of the Holy Spirit and the benefits of speaking in other tongues go hand in hand. Jesus said in John 16:7, "Nevertheless I tell you the truth. It is to your advantage that I go away; for if I do not go away, the Helper will not come to you; but if I depart, I will send Him to you."

In this portion of Scripture Jesus is getting ready to leave His disciples and go to be with His Father in heaven. He was telling them that it would be more beneficial for them that He goes, because then He would send to them the Holy Spirit. You see, Jesus was limited to His earthly body. He couldn't be everywhere at all times, whereas the Holy Spirit can be with each one of us, no matter where we are. Whether someone's in Thailand or India or here in Woodland Hills, Los Angeles, California, the Holy Spirit of God can be all over the place.

So Jesus said that it's more important that He go and that He send the Holy Spirit to His disciples—His disciples then and His disciples now. That's Peter, Paul, and Matthew in the New Testament, and that's you and me today!

Read what Jesus says in Mark 16:17 about speaking in tongues: "And these signs will follow those who believe: In My name they will cast out demons; they will speak with new tongues."

The gift of tongues then is for each and every person who calls himself a believer. Are you a believer? Then this gift is from God to you for your benefit.

At first in our Christian walk my husband, Mel, and I didn't speak in tongues. We had been baptized in the Holy Ghost and knew we had the gift, but because we didn't understand the benefits of it, it just seemed kind of silly to go around uttering what we thought was gibberish. Once we heard teaching on it, though, it was a whole new eye opening experience that would change us into being part of the 7 percent of the Christians that populate heaven and plunder hell while boldly proclaiming the good news of the gospel of Jesus Christ. We began speaking in tongues. And then we became fireball Christians. When you speak in other tongues, you're building yourself up on your most holy faith and igniting what's inside you to bring on the fire of God in your life.

Here are at least ten benefits of speaking in tongues:

1. You make yourself spiritually strong

Jude 1:20 says, "But you, beloved, building yourselves up on your most holy faith, praying in the Holy Spirit."

So you build yourself up when you pray in the Holy Ghost.

Not only do you build yourself up in your faith and encourage yourself, but also you edify yourself. First Corinthians 14:4 says, "He who speaks in a tongue edifies himself." Edify means to "enlighten, inform, educate, improve, educate, and teach." So while prophecy edifies the church, speaking in tongues edifies you. And you need to edify yourself. You need to build yourself up. You need to encourage yourself. Praying in tongues will do that.

I have found that prayer is the difference between success and failure. I believe that any failure in life can be traced back to a prayer failure. So I've learned to pray a situation through until it comes to pass, and often that requires me to pray in the Holy Spirit.

Praying in tongues creates a personal change in your life, and nothing you can do will benefit you more than this type of prayer.

2. You get delivered from the flesh

Have you ever wanted to do something, let's say go on a diet, and you say, "I'm never going to eat ice cream again. I'm not going to do it. I'm just going to eat foods that are healthy for me." So you cut up your raw vegetables, and after you've eaten your cauliflower and your broccoli and your carrots, you go out for a drive and spot a Dairy Queen. Oops! Well you weren't planning to, but all of a sudden you find yourself saying, "I'll have just one of those," and there you are eating this wonderfully swirled ice cream cone dipped in chocolate.

Maybe you drop by the mall and are tempted by a Mrs. Fields cookie. Can you relate? Well, that's the your flesh taking over what you had wanted to do. You had a great game plan with the lean proteins and grains and vegetables, but temptation got in your way.

Galatians 5:16–17 says, "I say then: Walk in the Spirit, and you shall not fulfill the lust of the flesh. For the flesh lusts against the Spirit, and the Spirit against the flesh; and these are contrary to one another, so that you do not do the things that you wish."

I desire to eat raw veggies every day, but I don't always do it. Why not? Because my flesh loves to eat sweets at times. So there's this battle that goes on. How do you not eat that thing that's in front of you? Is it all will-power? I'm telling you, there's a supernatural power to overcome that temptation if you will pray in tongues.

If you're having a problem with the lusts of the flesh, it's a direct sign that you need supernatural power that comes from praying in the Holy Spirit. When I first got this revelation about praying this way, I was anorexic and bulimic, even after I was saved. Anorexia is when you don't eat. Bulimia is when you eat then get so mad at yourself that you throw up all your food and take diuretics and laxatives.

I started to hear teaching about the power of the Holy Spirit and praying in tongues. So one day I just decided to go ahead and make the cookie dough that I loved and give the praying in tongues thing a try. As I was getting ready to devour the cookie dough, I began to pray in the Spirit, and the most supernatural thing happened. The power of the Holy Spirit was so strong in the room that I literally felt God's presence all over me. I got down on my knees and worshiped God. When I got back up, I was a changed, transformed person and was able to take that junk food I was going to binge on and throw it all away. For a binge eater, this was a miracle. So that was my first taste of the power of the Holy Spirit in my life.

Now, willpower might keep you from buying something not good for you to eat, but once it's in your hand, it takes more than willpower to throw that thing away. So I began to find out that there was something to praying in other tongues. My advice is for people to pray in the Holy Spirit for several minutes a day for a week and see if it's life changing. If it's not, why do it? But I believe you'll start to see supernatural signs and wonders happen in your life as you take advantage of this amazing free gift God has given to you.

I was completely, 100 percent, healed from anorexia and bulimia. And I give all the glory to God and the teachings from His Word. As we read the Word, we find out that the Word is Jesus. So reading God's Word gives us revelation of Jesus Christ and how to live our lives with Him as our example.

It's been over thirty years since I've been completely healed of eating disorders. So there's something powerful and real to this type of prayer.

I like to use this food illustration because most of us can relate to eating. But you can use any area in your life where you're having a challenge with the lusts of the flesh. I encourage you to pray in the Holy Spirit and to renew your mind through the Word of God. Experience the supernatural power that's available to every believer as you pray in other tongues.

3. The Holy Spirit will teach and remind you

John 14:26 says, "But the Helper, the Holy Spirit, whom the Father will send in My name, He will teach you all things, and bring to your remembrance all things that I said to you."

How many times have you read Scripture and then forgotten everything you've read? When Mel and I started leading people to the Lord and getting them saved, we started praying in the Holy Spirit. All of a sudden there would be this divine appointment with somebody, and I'd think, "Oh, I wish I could remember certain scriptures," but I could not seem to recall them. Then all of a sudden the Word of God would rise up and come out of my mouth, feeling like it was bypassing my brain. I would find myself quoting all of these wonderful verses, all the while thinking, "Wow, this is amazing that I am remembering these scriptures so easily. Where are all these words coming from?" Reading the Scripture passage two days earlier had logged it into my memory, and the Holy Spirit was bringing it forth just at the time it was needed. I couldn't have done that on my own. Later I realized that praying in tongues that morning had prepared me for that divine afternoon setup by God.

Now I can quote all these scriptures even though I'm not a chapter-and-verse person. How? The Holy Spirit is alive inside of me, and He's alive inside of you. And He can speak through you when you allow Him to. When you're praying in other tongues, you're stirring up these giftings, and He brings all things to remembrance. What a miracle!

4. You speak to God

First Corinthians 14:2 says, "For he who speaks in a tongue does not speak to men but to God, for no one understands him; however, in the spirit he speaks mysteries."

Have you ever just wanted to praise God because you love Him so, and you find yourself saying things like "Praise You, Lord," "I love You, Father," or "God, You're so awesome"? But you just don't have enough words to express yourself to Him. This is where the gift of praying in other tongues comes in, where you can continue to worship Him in the Holy Spirit.

5. You'll receive help when you don't know what to do

During my career in stunt work, I had a couple of near-death experiences, and during those times I cried out in the Holy Spirit to my Father in heaven. In an incident I mentioned to you earlier in the Coca-Cola commercial when the airplane was diving toward the ground, while I didn't know all of the details of what was going on with the plane, I did know that I could cry out to my heavenly Father in other tongues. I knew that He would intervene on my behalf, whether it was to send a dozen angels or one angel to fix whatever needed to be fixed. Maybe it was to work through the pilot to give him the wisdom of God. Whatever needed to be taken care of, I knew that if I prayed in tongues, God would take care of it. And He did!

Remember Romans 8:26: "Likewise the Spirit also helps in our weaknesses. For we do not know what we should pray for as we ought, but the Spirit Himself makes intercessions for us with groanings which cannot be uttered."

How many times have you prayed for someone's salvation, but they didn't get saved? Or maybe you prayed for their healing, but they didn't get healed. Well, you don't know what's keeping them from getting saved or healed. Maybe there's a root of bitterness or unforgiveness in their lives. There are all sorts of reasons why their miracle isn't happening. But as you're praying in other tongues, you're praying the perfect prayer for what their needs are. That's why you can pray everything you know how to pray for in English, but to get the breakthrough you may need to go into other tongues. Now you're getting into the area of the supernatural ways of God.

6. He will guide you into all truth

John 16:13 says, "However, when He, the Spirit of truth, has come, He will guide you into all truth; for He will not speak on His own authority, but whatever He hears He will speak; and He will tell you things to come."

I've found that if I've been spending a lot of time praying in the Holy Spirit, sometimes hours a day, I become extra sensitive to what's going on around me because I'm sensitive in the spirit realm; if somebody tells me a lie, it's like an alarm goes off inside me. While I may not know for sure if they're telling me the truth or not, my spirit senses something isn't right. When this happens to you, the Holy Spirit within you, who is truth and guides you into all truth, alerts you to something that is contrary to the truth.

7. You will receive power

With God's supernatural power, we can do more good in the world, and we're able to help more people than we can without it.

Jesus says in Acts 1:8, "But you shall receive power when the Holy Spirit has come upon you; and you shall be witnesses to Me in Jerusalem, and in all Judea and Samaria, and to the end of the earth." That means that you'll be a witness wherever you go.

Romans 8:11 says, "But if the Spirit of Him who raised

Jesus from the dead dwells in you, He who raised Christ from the dead will also give life to your mortal bodies through His Spirit who dwells in you."

Now this is powerful news from the Word of God. And you have to believe that this is for you. You deserve every gift God has for you. He says in His Word that He's not going to withhold any good gift from His children (Ps. 84:11) and that He's no respecter of persons, because He doesn't show partiality (Acts 10:34).

Unfortunately, many in the body of Christ have trouble receiving the gift of speaking in tongues. Often it's because they have been brought up in a church that told them, "Speaking in other tongues is from the devil," "You just shouldn't do it," or "It's not for the church today." That's sad, because we can see according to Scripture that's just not the truth. The truth is, the apostle Paul said he wished that all spoke in tongues (1 Cor. 14:5). He said that he spoke in tongues more than any of the others (v. 18). He was encouraging people to stir up the gift of speaking in tongues that was inside them. They were being admonished to imitate him as he imitated Christ.

8. You will be a witness

We've already read Acts 1:8, but I want to share it one more time: "But you shall receive power when the Holy Spirit has come upon you; and you shall be witnesses to Me in Jerusalem, and in all Judea and Samaria, and to the end of the earth."

We've talked about the power that shows up when the Holy Spirit comes upon you, but you'll also be a witness, which is so much of the joy of being a Christian. The highest high you will ever experience is leading someone to the Lord, testifying of His goodness in your life, and being a witness for the glory of God.

So when you pray in the Holy Ghost, you're stirring yourself up, and you become a witness for Christ to those around you.

9. You will have dreams and visions and get to see the good things God has for you

Acts 2:17–18 tells us: "And it shall come to pass in the last days, says God, that I will pour out of My Spirit on all flesh; your sons and your daughters shall prophesy, your young men shall see visions, your old men shall dream dreams. And on My menservants and on My maidservants I will pour out My Spirit in those days; and they shall prophesy."

First Corinthians 2:9–10 says, "But as it is written: 'Eye has not seen, nor ear heard, nor have entered into the heart of man the things which God has prepared for those who love Him.' But God has revealed them to us through His Spirit. For the Spirit searches all things, yes, the deep things of God."

As you're praying in the Holy Spirit, you're going to be stirring up spiritual giftings. You will begin to see things that God has planned for your future that He desires to come to pass. You're going to start knowing things before they happen. You're going to have such a tuned-in relationship with God that if you're not to drive down a certain street because there will be a bomb going off or a drive-by shooting, He will prompt you to go this way and you will know, because you're in tune to the voice of the Holy Spirit. You have a relationship with Him, and you can feel Him.

When I feel the Holy Spirit telling me something

and I disobey, it's like a grieving inside me. I get little twinges in my stomach and I know I'm doing the wrong thing. For example, if I start to go a certain direction in a conversation, I can feel a grieving in my spirit as though I'm doing something that will disappoint the Holy Spirit, either by what I'm listening to or by what I'm saying. I know that I'd better back up quickly, because I'm in dangerous territory when I grieve the Holy Spirit.

The Bible tells us in Ephesians 4:30, "And do not grieve the Holy Spirit of God, by whom you were sealed for the day of redemption." The Holy Spirit is my Comforter, my Counselor, the One who is going to lead me and guide me into all truth. I do not want to grieve the Holy Spirit. Now when I've done the right thing, this overwhelming peace and joy of the Holy Ghost is all over me.

10. You get a helper forever

Jesus' words in John 14:16–17 tell us, "And I will pray the Father, and He will give you another Helper, that He may abide with you forever—the Spirit of truth, whom the world cannot receive, because it neither sees Him nor knows Him; but you know Him, for He dwells with you and will be in you."

Isn't it wonderful to know that you have the best Helper and Counselor in your life, and that He's there 24/7? What a wonderful gift God has given each one of us. He will tell us what to do in the tough times.

Here's a humorous story that illustrates God being there for us. A tourist came too close to the edge of the Grand Canyon, lost his footing, and plunged over the side, clawing and scratching to save himself. After he went out of sight and just before he fell into space, he encountered a scrubby bush, which he desperately grabbed with both hands. Filled with terror, he called out toward heaven, "Is there anyone up there?" A calm, powerful voice came out of the sky, "Yes, there is." The tourist pleaded, "Can you help me? Can you help me?" The calm voice replied, "Yes, I probably can. What is your problem?" The tourist replied, "I fell over a cliff and am dangling in space, holding on to a bush that is about to let go. Please, help me!" The voice from above said, "I'll try. Do you believe?" "Yes, yes, I believe!" "Do you have faith?" "Yes, yes, I have strong faith." The calm voice said, "Well, in that case, simply let loose of the bush, and everything will turn out fine." There was a pause, then the tourist yelled, "Is there anyone else up there?"

God may not speak to you in an audible voice as He did to the tourist in our story, but He just might speak to you in a still small voice on the inside of you letting you know right from wrong, leading and guiding you as you follow His direction.

I want to leave you with a few guidelines to help you develop your gift of praying in the Holy Spirit:

- Try praying in the Holy Spirit several minutes a day for a week. If it's life changing, do it for the rest of your life.

- Increase your time of praying in the Holy Spirit during any spiritual battles you encounter.

- Look for opportunities to pray in the Holy Spirit when you're driving, exercising, cleaning, you name it.

- After you pray in the Holy Spirit, ask the Lord to give you in English what you prayed, and then record your prayer in a journal.

Here are a few snares of the enemy to watch for when you're exercising your gift of praying in tongues:

- You may think thoughts like, "What you are doing is silly." That thought is from the devil, because he does not want you to have this power gift!

- You may feel like what you're doing isn't making any difference. The truth is, it is making a difference, keep doing it!

- You may even think that you're making up the sounds that are coming out of your mouth.

While almost everyone feels at one time or another all of the above, I want to encourage you to develop your gift of speaking in tongues. Praying in tongues is just another step in your walk of faith. The Bible clearly shows the power of this type of prayer; therefore I am going to do it. I pray that you'll be blessed as you do too, and that you'll enjoy living a supernatural life in a natural world.

To receive the Holy Spirit, pray this simple prayer:

Dear Father God, I believe that You sent Jesus to die on the cross and to be raised from the dead. Jesus, come into my heart and be my Lord and Savior. Forgive me for every sin that I have done. I forgive

*everyone who has hurt me...I let it go. Bless them,
Lord. Fill me with Your Holy Spirit, with the evidence of speaking in other tongues and every gift
that You have. Thank You, Lord. I believe and I
receive.*

Now that you prayed that prayer, all you have to do
is open your mouth and let whatever sound wants to
come out...and simply flow with it.

I pray for His power and gifting to flow through your
life, making you a world shaker and history maker for
the glory of God!

If you prayed the prayer for the first time, I would
love to hear from you. Please write me, so I can send
you more information and pray for you.

5

PUT YOUR COMPLETE
HEART TRUST IN GOD

B ELIEVE ME; I had to trust God completely on the day of my accident. First of all, when they put me in a helicopter to transport me from the movie set location in the desert to the Sherman Oaks Burn Center, someone on the medical staff started shooting me full of morphine. Unfortunately, I had an allergic reaction to the drug and began throwing up. I had to tell them not to give me any more drugs, which meant I had to trust God totally to get me through this ordeal with no painkillers.

While I had no idea what was happening and what the outcome was going to be, I had to believe that God was going to get me through this situation. I knew He would comfort me, because His Word tells me that the Holy Spirit is my Comforter. But I had to make a choice to put my complete heart trust in Him.

God wants our 100 percent heart trust. Not 97 percent or 98 percent, but complete 100 percent heart trust in Him. Again we recall from Scripture the admonition in Proverbs 3:5–6 to trust in the Lord with all of our heart and not to lean on our own understanding. And there's a promise that goes along with this. God tells us that if we will acknowledge Him in all our ways, then He will direct our paths.

What Does It Mean to Trust?

The first definition in my dictionary for the word trust is: "assured reliance on the character, ability, strength, or truth of someone or something." It also means to "be confident, to hope, to commit one's care or keeping, to entrust, to believe."

Here's what the Bible tells us about putting our complete heart trust in God:

> So trust in the Lord (commit yourself to Him, lean on Him, hope confidently in Him) forever; for the Lord God is an everlasting Rock [the Rock of Ages].
>
> —Isaiah 26:4, amp

Now let's look at other scriptures that list just a few of the benefits of totally and completely trusting in God:

Your battles will be won

> And they [the Israelites] were helped against them, and the Hagrites were delivered into their hand, and all who were with them, for they cried out to God in the battle. He heeded their prayer, because they put their trust in Him.
>
> —1 Chronicles 5:20

You will be happy, blessed, and fortunate

> He who heeds the word wisely will find good, and whoever trusts in the Lord, happy is he.
>
> —Proverbs 16:20

You will be safe from deadly plagues and diseases

I will say of the Lord, "He is my refuge and my fortress; my God, in Him I will trust." Surely He shall deliver you from the snare of the fowler and from the perilous pestilence.

—PSALM 91:2–3

You will have no fear

You shall not be afraid of the terror by night, nor of the arrow that flies by day.

—PSALM 91:5

Your body will be healthy

Trust in the Lord with all your heart, and lean not on your own understanding; in all your ways acknowledge Him, and He shall direct your paths....It will be health to your flesh, and strength to your bones.

—PROVERBS 3:5–6, 8

God will be your shield

As for God, His way is perfect; the word of the Lord is proven. He is a shield to all who trust in Him.

—PSALM 18:30

God will be your refuge

Trust in Him at all times, you people; pour out your heart before Him; God is a refuge for us.

—PSALM 62:8

You will be safe and set on high

The fear of man brings a snare, but whoever trusts in the Lord shall be safe.

—Proverbs 29:25

You will prosper

He who is of a proud heart stirs up strife, but he who trusts in the Lord will be prospered.

—Proverbs 28:25

You will be delivered and saved from the wicked

And the Lord shall help them and deliver them; He shall deliver them from the wicked, and save them, because they trust in Him.

—Psalm 37:40

You will be safe from your persecutors

Show Your marvelous lovingkindness by Your right hand, O You who save those who trust in You from those who rise up against them.

—Psalm 17:7

God will be a covering and defense for you

But let all those rejoice who put their trust in You; let them ever shout for joy, because You defend them; let those also who love Your name be joyful in You.

—Psalm 5:11

You will experience God's goodness

> Oh, how great is Your goodness, which You have laid up for those who fear You, which You have prepared for those who trust in You in the presence of the sons of men!
>
> —PSALM 31:19

He will bring to pass the desires of your heart

> Trust in the Lord, and do good; dwell in the land, and feed on His faithfulness. Delight yourself also in the Lord, and He shall give you the desires of your heart.
>
> —PSALM 37:3–4

Now that we've read some of the benefits of trusting totally in the Lord, and should be convinced there are many good things in store for those who do, let's look at ways to help us rely on Him completely.

TRUSTING GOD FOR OUR CALL

Mel and I currently co-pastor In His Presence Church located in Woodland Hills, Los Angeles, California. Starting a church from scratch with no money takes trusting God, believe me.

It would have been easy to take a more glamorous road. For example, many other opportunities presented themselves, like a co-pastoring position in Tampa, Florida, where Mel grew up. Another position in Florida was offered to us where we would have a home, a boat, and a plot of land provided to build a church. Right here in California, in Chatsworth, we were offered land that held three churches for us to pastor. A home was also on the property, and we were offered a nice salary.

But both Mel and I knew that God had called us to start a church led by His Holy Spirit, where we would be in a position to do whatever God told us. So our garage in Van Nuys became our office. Our living room became our church prayer room. Our backyard became the classroom for new members. Now this all took a lot of trusting in God to meet all of the needs that were required to begin a new work for Him.

Currently we have a beautiful forty-thousand-square-foot building that houses comfortable offices, quiet prayer rooms, and a lovely sanctuary. A peaceful waterfall greets all who enter the church. It's a place where approximately fifty people a week give their hearts to Jesus. As we were faithful to what we believed God was calling us to do in building In His Presence Church, God has been faithful to us. Second Chronicles 16:9 tells us, "For the eyes of the Lord run to and fro throughout the whole earth, to show Himself strong on behalf of those whose heart is loyal to Him."

Trust in God, Not in People

The Bible makes it clear that we are not to completely trust man. Psalm 146:3 tells us, "Put not your trust in princes, nor in a son of man, in whom there is no help." Jeremiah 17:5 says, "Thus says the Lord: 'Cursed is the man who trusts in man and makes flesh his strength, whose heart departs from the Lord.'" On the contrary, verse 7 says, "Blessed is the man who trusts in the Lord, and whose hope is the Lord."

Here's a humorous example of what happens when we put out trust in man instead of God:

There were three ministers who decided to put their trust in one another. They pastored three different churches in the same town and decided to go fishing and share with one another their sins.

The first pastor said, "Do you know what my big sin is? My big sin is drinking. I know it's wrong, but every Friday night I drive to a city where no one will recognize me, and I go to a saloon and get drunk. I know I shouldn't, but I can't help it. That's my big sin."

The second pastor said, "Well, fellas, to be honest with you, I've got a big sin too. My big sin is gambling. As a matter of fact, you know all the money I raised for that mission trip to India? I took it to Las Vegas instead and lost it all. I'm so ashamed. But that's my big sin."

Finally the third pastor's turn came around. He said, "Guys, I probably should have gone first, because my big sin is gossiping."

VICTORY COMES FROM TRUSTING GOD

I can testify to the victory that God brings when we trust in Him 100 percent. At the time of my accident, I chose to put my complete heart trust in Him. Because I did, He brought me through many painful times during my ten-day stay in the hospital and healed me totally of my burns.

There did come a time in the process of my healing that I needed to make a choice of whether or not to have skin grafted from other parts of my body to put on my upper lip, ear, and wrist. But since so much miracle power had taken place up to that point, I wondered what having that procedure done would do to my testimony.

I felt that I looked fine, but my doctor suggested that if I ever planned to be on television again, I should seriously consider having the skin graft.

I prayed about what to do and was having a hard time, until I heard God say, "Desiree, it's not a matter of whether to get the grafting or not to get the grafting. It's a matter of your heart, in just trusting Me in whatever decision you make. It's your decision at this point, but keep your heart trust in Me."

Mel and I decided to go ahead with the grafting, so the surgeon took skin from the back of my head and put some on my upper lip, left ear, and right wrist. I know of burn victims who have had numerous amounts of skin grafting and still have tremendous scarring. I have no scarring other than a little mark on my right wrist that reminds me how good and how faithful God was to heal me when my entire face should be scarred for life.

I believe this is important for people to know. Whether or not you decide to take chemo treatments, for example, or any other treatment doctors may be prescribing, God cares that you put your complete heart trust in Him. Taking medication or having surgery does not mean that you don't trust God for your healing. He can bring you victory in many ways. The important thing is that you trust Him for the outcome.

Here are three things to remember in learning to put your complete heart trust in God:

1. Draw near to God, and He will draw near to you.

2. Watch and pray; pray and obey.

3. Trust what He says in His Word.

And remember Jesus' words to His followers when He told them to go into all the world and make disciples of the nations. He told them that He would never leave them or forsake them; He would be with them always (Matt. 28:19–20). The principle here holds true no matter what we do as followers of Christ. Whether we are out on the streets evangelizing or going through a difficult period of life, Jesus will never leave us or forsake us. He will be with us always. You can put your complete heart trust in that promise!

6

CALL IN THE GENERALS

WHILE I WAS still lying in the dirt on the movie set, before the helicopter arrived to transport me to the Sherman Oaks Burn Center, the assistant director came over to me and asked whom he could telephone for me. "Please call my husband. He needs to start praying for me." I also told him to call my dad. "He'll pray for me." My dad had prayed for me for ten years before I came to know Jesus. He'd been my faithful prayer warrior all those years. I knew he would be faithful to pray for me now.

In my time of crisis, I needed and wanted strong men and women of God to surround me. And they did. They were people I would consider to be generals in the spiritual realm. I define a spiritual general this way: someone who knows how to pray the Word of God and live it. My two special generals were my husband and my dad, the two men who I knew loved me more than anybody else in the world.

I thank God that during my time of need, when I couldn't even use my hands because they were too weak to pick up my Bible, I had generals I could count on to pick up the Bible and read it to me, pray for me, and to lift me up to God's throne room of grace and mercy.

Ecclesiastes 4:9–10 tells us, "Two are better than one, because they have a good return for their work: If one falls down, his friend can help him up. But pity the man who falls and has no one to help him up!" (NIV).

Mel and my dad took shifts in my hospital room to make sure I was covered in prayer at all times. They were determined that God's Word would be spoken over me around the clock. In fact, they brought in tapes of the Bible and praise music so that I could enter into the presence of God and spend my entire day and night there. During those ten days in the hospital, I just wanted 100 percent God. And you know, if you're going for a full-blown miracle, you need to be consumed with God.

Nothing else is going to bring complete healing to your situation—not television programs, not the radio, nothing but the Word of God and His presence to saturate and cleanse your mind, your heart, and every part of your body.

THE REAL ENEMY

Since our fight is not against flesh, but against principalities, against powers, against the rulers of the darkness of this age, against spiritual hosts of wickedness in the heavenly places, as Paul writes in Ephesians 6:12, our greatest weapon is prayer. That's why I recommend calling in the prayer generals in times of crisis. I certainly did following my accident. I needed my generals to be strong for me.

As I stated earlier, when Mel arrived at the hospital,

he took one look at me and started to cry. And I thought, "Oh, no, this is bad." I hadn't seen myself yet, so I didn't know what kind of damage had been done. But he'd look at me and just weep. My dad took one look at me and started to cry. In fact, almost everyone that saw me in the first three days of my hospital stay, cried. I knew by their reactions that I had been hurt badly and needed a miracle from God.

But all the tears told me that my prayer warriors had a lot of work ahead of them. Prayer is the key that unlocks the storehouse of God's infinite grace and power. All that God is and all that God has for His children is at the disposal of prayer. I was in need of a miracle, and I needed the army of Christ to pray on my behalf.

Many Christian soldiers would just march into my hospital room with a word or a scripture, and they'd pray for me. They'd say that God had sent them to share a specific nugget, and it was always something I needed to hear right at that moment. I love the body of Christ. I love those who will stand in the gap for those in need.

One strong Christian soldier who was a friend of my dad (a prayer warrior in his eighties) came marching into my room and said that God had sent him. After reading the Bible and praying for me, he said that he had a specific word from heaven for me. "Desiree, God wants you to just open your heart and receive." I knew it was God speaking to me through this man. I could feel my heart opening to God, and His love and healing power filled me up that day. A tremendous part of my miracle took place right then. I barely knew the man, but he was a faithful soldier in the army of God.

Other faithful Christian soldiers in the body of Christ called TBN and CBN (major Christian TV networks) that have prayer warriors available. They put me on their lists to be prayed for. My dad attended a meeting with Charles and Frances Hunter, the Happy Hunters, long known in the body of Christ for their healing ministry, and the whole group prayed for me that night. Many others in Bible studies and prayer meetings around the nation prayed for me as my faithful brothers and sisters in Christ made phone calls asking for prayer on my behalf.

I encourage you to have relationships with people who will go the distance spiritually for you in your time of need. Mentally make a list of them, so that when you're in a crisis, you can call in the generals! The best places to meet these powerful prayer warriors are churches that teach the Bible and prayer and that believe in and expect to see miracles, signs, and wonders in the world today.

I am so grateful for those in the body of Christ who prayed fervently for me. Choose friends who pray, and be a friend who prays.

7

STAND ON GOD'S WORD

DURING MY TIME in the hospital I didn't want the television going, I didn't want to read magazines, and I didn't want to visit. All I wanted was to saturate myself in the Word of God, because I knew it was there that I would find help in my time of need. I clung to the truth in Proverbs 4:20–22 where God says, "My son, give attention to my words; incline your ear to my sayings. Do not let them depart from your eyes; keep them in the midst of your heart; for *they are life to those who find them, and health to all their flesh*" (emphasis added).

HEARING THE WORD 24/7

We literally had the Word of God being read or played on the cassette player 24/7 in my hospital room. People would take turns reading the Bible over me, or I would have my tapes going, and I would just meditate on the Word. At this point I still couldn't use my hands to pick up my Bible or work the buttons on my tape player, so visitors would put my tapes on for me, and when they'd leave, I'd just continue to listen to the Word. I was hearing the Scriptures over and over and building my faith, because the Bible says that faith comes by hearing and hearing by the Word of God (Rom. 10:17).

I believed then, and I do now, that if God says something in His Word, then it's true. That's just the way it is. I like this acronym for BIBLE: Basic Instructions Before Leaving Earth. Did you know that you can base your whole life on the Bible? I know that because of what God says in His Word.

Because I knew the Proverbs passage at the beginning of this chapter and Psalm 107:20, which says, "He sent His word and healed them," I knew I could stand on God's Word for my miracle healing.

Also, I was familiar with Jeremiah 1:12, which says that God is watching over His Word to perform it in my life. Likewise, Isaiah 55:11 says, "So shall My word be that goes forth from My mouth; it shall not return to Me void, but it shall accomplish what I please, and it shall prosper in the thing for which I sent it."

These verses and many others were lifelines for me during my hospital stay. So every day the Word of God was either being spoken over me or read to me, or I listened to it on tape.

This was not my first time believing that the Word of God would heal me. I remember one time when I was doing stunt work in a horror movie. Can you believe I was a Christian and doing horror flicks? Back then, in the peak of my career, I worked every day on some film, TV show, or commercial. I had an answering service that all the top-working stunt people had back then called Teddy's. The studios would give me a call to see if I was available to work the next day or week for a certain stunt coordinator, and if I said yes, they'd tell me something like this: "Report to Universal Studios at 6:00 a.m. on

Stage 24... or Fox Studios on stage 11," or other locations. Often I didn't even know what the show was, or which actress I would be the stunt double for.

On this particular assignment, as a young Christian, I found myself in quite a predicament. In the scene I was being chased by a monster. I'd have to run through this long cave where a dog would be dead and hanging by his nose from the top of the cave. Half a man's body would be lying on the ground with an axe through it. Yuck! Of course, these were all pretend movie items, but they looked so real. That day I had my first full-blown migraine headache and would be in so much pain that I'd run to the bathroom, get sick and throw up, and then go back and do my scene all over again. I tried not to let anyone know how sick I was. The call time was 6:00 a.m., but around midnight I was still being chased by this seven-foot monster.

In part of the scene I was climbing up a rope in a well trying to escape. I would get almost to the top and would hang there, and the monster would swing me into the sides of the well, banging my body against the walls. All the while my head was throbbing. I arrived home at two thirty in the morning in tears. Around 6:00 a.m. I told my husband that the pain was unbearable and that I just wanted to die. At that point he started firing away healing scriptures. He said, "Desiree, you need to act on your faith; get up and walk!" he commanded. I just lay there and said that I couldn't move. He said, "We're going to walk around the block."

I thought he was crazy when he grabbed my hands, threw a bathrobe on me, took me outside, and began walking me around the block. Mel insisted that I walk and repeat scriptures after him. I did, and, believe it or not, halfway around the block I was completely healed! Glory to God!

So, in essence, I had been prepared to know what to expect following my accident. I had already experienced victory in the Word of God. I knew that His Word heals.

In what area of your life do you need healing or release? Let me walk you around the spiritual block. Please say these healing scriptures out loud:

- By His stripes I am healed (1 Pet. 2:24).

- I'm redeemed from the hand of the foe (Ps. 107:2).

- I'm delivered from the powers of darkness and translated into God's kingdom (Col. 1:13).

- I am more than a conqueror (Rom. 8:37).

- I'm an overcomer by the blood of the Lamb and the word of my testimony (Rev. 12:11).

- I am walking by faith and not by sight (2 Cor. 5:7).

- I am God's child, for I am born again of the incorruptible seed of the Word of God, which lives and abides forever (1 Pet. 1:23).

- I am forgiven of all my sins and washed in the blood (Eph. 1:7; Col. 1:14; Heb. 9:14; 1 John 2:12).

- I am a new creature (2 Cor. 5:17).

- I am the temple of the Holy Spirit (1 Cor. 6:19).

- I am blessed (Deut. 28:1–14; Gal. 3:9).

- I am a saint (Rom. 1:7; 1 Cor. 1:2; Phil. 1:1).

- I am the head and not the tail, above only and not beneath (Deut. 28:13).

- I am holy and without blame before Him in love (Eph. 1:4; 1 Pet. 1:15).

- I am victorious (Rev. 21:7).

- I am set free (John 8:31–33).

- I am strong in the Lord (Eph. 6:10).

- I am free from condemnation (Rom. 8:1).

- I am firmly rooted, built up, established in my faith, and overflowing with gratitude (Col. 2:7).

- I am born of God, and the evil one does not touch me (1 John 5:18).

- I am His faithful follower (Eph. 5:1; Rev. 17:14).

- I am overtaken with blessings (Deut. 28:2; Eph. 1:3).

- I am His disciple because I have love for others (John 13:34–35).

- I am the light of the world and the salt of the earth (Matt. 5:13–14).

- I am the righteousness of God in Christ Jesus (2 Cor. 5:21).

- I am a partaker of His divine nature (2 Pet. 1:4).

- I am called of God (2 Tim. 1:9).

- I am chosen (Eph. 1:4; 1 Thess. 1:4; 1 Pet. 2:9).

- I am an ambassador for Christ (2 Cor. 5:20).

- I am God's workmanship, created in Christ Jesus for good works (Eph. 2:10).

- I am the apple of my heavenly Father's eye (Deut. 32:10; Ps. 17:8).

- I am being changed into His image (2 Cor. 3:18; Phil. 1:6).

- I am raised up with Christ and seated in heavenly places (Eph. 2:6; Col. 2:12).

- I am beloved of God (Col. 3:12; 1 Thess. 1:4).

- I am one in Christ (John 17:21–23).

- I have the mind of Christ (1 Cor. 2:16; Phil. 2:5).

- I have overcome the world (1 John 5:4).

- I have everlasting life and will not be condemned (John 5:24; 6:47).

- I have the peace of God, which passes all understanding (Phil. 4:7).

- I have received the power of the Holy Spirit to lay hands on the sick and see them recover, power to cast out demons,

power over all the power of the enemy,
and nothing shall by any means hurt me
(Mark 16:17–18).

- I can do all things through Christ Jesus
  (Phil. 4:13).

- I shall do even greater works than these in
  Christ Jesus (John 5:20).

- I possess the greater One in me, because
  greater is He who is in me than he who is
  in the world (1 John 4:4).

- I press toward the mark for the prize of
  the high calling of God (Phil. 3:14).

- I always triumph in Christ (2 Cor. 2:14).

What the Word Will Do for You

We've already looked at Psalm 107:20 and found that the
Word of God will heal you. The following are other benefits you'll enjoy from the Word:

The Word will guide you

Psalm 119:105 states, "Your word is a lamp to my feet
and a light to my path."

Do you have a decision to make? Do you need to
make a plan of action? Are you questioning some things
that are going on in your life? Read the Word. It will
bring illumination and direction.

The Word will bring you success

Joshua 1:8 says, "This Book of the Law shall not depart
from your mouth, but you shall meditate on it day and
night, that you may observe to do according to all that

is written in it. For then you will make your way prosperous, and then you will have good success."

Are you tired of working on projects that seem to fail? Do you want to flourish in your work? Would you like to succeed in reaching life goals? Read the Word. It will prosper you and bring you success.

The Word will sustain you

Matthew 4:4 says, "It is written, 'Man shall not live by bread alone, but by every word that proceeds from the mouth of God.'"

The Lord had already shown Himself strong with the Word of God in my life when He healed me of anorexia and bulimia, so I learned to find certain scriptures in the Bible, like Matthew 4:4, that seemed to jump off the pages at me. God will do that for you too. As you read your Bible, look for verses that speak directly to you. Underline them, copy them into a journal, and memorize them. Store them in your heart; they will be life to you.

When my accident happened, I knew I could trust God and turn to the same principles from before for the miracle healing that I now so desperately needed.

When nothing seems to be working, and you're hungry for more in your life, read the Word. It will uphold you in the hard times and bring strength when you need it.

The Word will bring you satisfaction

John 4:14 tells us, "Whoever drinks of the water that I shall give him will never thirst. But the water that I shall give him will become in him a fountain of water springing up into everlasting life."

Romans 13:14 says, "But clothe yourself with the Lord

Jesus Christ (the Messiah), and make no provision for [indulging] the flesh [put a stop to thinking about the evil cravings of your physical nature] to [gratify its] desire (lusts)" (AMP).

Are you looking for fulfillment in your relationships, in your work, in your possessions? Read the Word and be filled to overflowing in the areas that really matter.

The Word will encourage you

Isaiah 41:10 reads, "Fear not, for I am with you; be not dismayed, for I am your God. I will strengthen you, yes, I will help you. I will uphold you with My righteous right hand."

Hebrews 13:6 states, "The Lord is my helper; I will not fear."

Is there something in your life that's making you fearful? Read the Word. Your God is with you. He will help you and uphold you.

The Word will comfort you

Psalm 119:50 says, "This is my comfort in my affliction, for Your word has given me life."

Paul wrote in 2 Thessalonians 2:16–17, "Now may our Lord Jesus Christ Himself, and our God and Father, who has loved us and given us everlasting consolation and good hope by grace, comfort your hearts and establish you in every good word and work."

Are you grieving the loss of a loved one? Have you found yourself without a job? Are you feeling forsaken by a friend? Read the Word. It will comfort you in your affliction, and it will give you hope.

The Word will bless you

Acts 3:25–26 says, "You are sons of the prophets, and of the covenant which God made with our father, saying to Abraham, 'And in your seed all the families of the earth shall be blessed.' To you first, God, having raised up His Servant Jesus, sent Him to bless you, in turning away every one of you from your iniquities."

Do you need approval? Are you feeling insignificant? Turn to God's Word. He wants to bless you and make you a blessing to others.

Get Into the Word and Get the Word Into You

The Word of God is like an arsenal. It's power when you feel weak, hope when you feel hopeless, and healing to your flesh. But here's where your part comes in. In order to have your arsenal full and ready to use when you need it, you need to make a choice to get into the Word and get the Word into you.

Since Mel and I already knew what God's Word said about healing, we immediately were able to stand on His promises for my miracle healing after the accident. Early on in our Christian walk we began to spend hours and hours in the Word, and we had the Word in us. So when we needed to call upon it, it was there, buried in our hearts.

Here are five ways to get into the Word and to get the Word into you:

1. Read the Word

2. Meditate on the Word

3. Memorize the Word

4. Remember the Word

5. Speak the Word

I encourage you to start out your days in the Word. Learn life's lessons the easy way. Daily hear His voice first thing every morning.

Jesus told us in Matthew 6:33, "Seek first the kingdom of God and His righteousness, and all these things shall be added to you."

FATHER OF FAITH STANDS ON GOD'S WORD

When Kenneth Hagin, the father of the Faith Movement, was sixteen years old, he was terminally ill. He only weighed eighty-nine pounds and was too sick and weak to even bathe or dress himself. His mama had to do it for him. He was so ill, in fact, that the doctors had given up on his recovery.

But young Hagin got his Bible and found himself a Scripture promise, a word from God to stand on. He chose Mark 11:22–24, which says, "And Jesus answering saith unto them, Have faith in God [the Greek says, have the faith of God]. For verily I say unto you, That whosoever shall say unto this mountain, be thou removed and be thou cast into the sea; and shall not doubt in his heart, but shall believe that those things which he saith shall come to pass; he shall have whatsoever he saith. Therefore I say unto you, What things so ever ye desire, when ye pray, believe that ye receive them, and ye shall have them" (KJV).

Pastor Hagin testified later in life that believing that he had received what he had asked for when he prayed, even though he hadn't yet seen the manifestation of it, was the key to receiving his healing of a terminal blood disease and heart condition that he had contracted more than sixty-five years earlier. He finally believed what God said in His Word over what his physical sense told him. And that brought him off a deathbed.

When he was there on that bed of sickness, he saw that he'd missed it by substituting hope for faith. He kept believing that he was going to get healed, and then he'd examine his body to see if he was healed. And if he could tell that he was healed, then he would believe he was healed.

He realized that he had to start believing he was healed while he was still lying there bedfast, unable to move an inch. He had to believe that he received his healing while his body was still paralyzed. He also saw that his part was to believe that he had received. God's part was to see that Kenneth had his healing.

What do you need today? Physical healing? Financial recovery? Relationship mending? Encouragement in your job? A career change? Whatever it is, find a Scripture promise to stand on. Then confess it, speak it over your situation, meditate on it, and, above all, believe it. Your Scripture verse is your weapon, your promise, your power, your faith. Believe it for yourself, and boldly declare it. Then watch how God performs His Word in your life.

Saturate yourself in the Word of God, stand on His promises, and get your miracle!

8

CLOSE THE DOOR
TO NEGATIVITY

SOMETIMES THE MOST well-meaning people can be the worst influence in the world for us. I had one stunt gal call me in the hospital. By this time I had strength enough to move my arms, so I could pick up the phone to answer it.

Most of the people in the body of Christ called with words of encouragement, but this gal called and said, "Oh, Desiree, you poor thing. I had my back burned once, and it was *soooo* painful. I know what you're going through."

Almost immediately I felt self-pity, sorrow, grief, and fear trying to take hold of me. I so badly wanted my miracle, and I knew that sympathy and words of sorrow would not help me. I could sense a tug-of-war going on inside me in those brief moments. Sure, I would have liked to cry and sob over the fact that my entire face and other parts of me were burned and that I felt tremendous pain. But I had made a decision not to be emotionally moved by what I felt. Rather I would keep my entire focus on Jesus, my Healer, my Source of strength, my Deliverer.

Listening to my phone caller's words of sympathy, I found myself shaking on the inside. I was so flustered that I simply dropped the phone to the floor and began to cry. My husband caught the receiver and responded that it was not a good time for me to talk. It took an hour or so of prayer and talking with my husband for me to shake off the effect of that phone call. Listen, sympathy will not heal. Faith in God will.

This stunt gal meant well, but what I needed to hear was the Word of God, not words of sympathy. I was standing for my miracle. I decided then that I needed to close the door to self-pity resulting in negativity.

If you're believing God for something, like a miracle healing, then you need to be careful about the people with whom you associate. Sometimes others can speak negative reports into your situation. Here you are trying to build your faith, and someone casts a negative word or thought at you. A word spoken like that can ring in your mind for a long time.

In times of crisis you need friends around you who will speak the Word of God into your situation. You need people who will remind you that by His stripes you are healed and to stand in faith with you.

Well, that day I told the nurses to unplug my phone and not to let any visitors in. I didn't want to see anybody. I just wanted to be alone with God and I was for a period of time. But somehow various Christians would make it into my room with just the right Scripture verse for me that day. I'm thankful to those who know when they are on divine assignment. When people are on assignment from God, they can get past anybody.

I remember a time when Mel and I were on a divine assignment to go and pray for someone in the hospital, but when we got there, we were told we couldn't go in because the man was in the intensive care unit, and only family members were allowed to visit. As we started to leave, I felt the tug of the Holy Spirit that we were supposed to pray for this man. So I told the nurses that I was his sister, which I was...in the Lord. So we got in, laid hands on the man, prayed over him, and, boom, he woke up out of his coma.

NEGATIVITY ON THE HOME FRONT

Sometimes we need to close the door to negativity even with people really close to us. For example, one day I was stressed and got negative with Mel while we were talking on our cell phones. All of a sudden I began to hear this noise that sounded like static, and Mel saying, "Breaking up...breaking up...can't hear you," in a kidding tone of voice. Then the phone went dead.

I started laughing when I realized what had just happened. I was glad that Mel had hung up on me. Now, he doesn't recommend hanging up on your mate, but that day I deserved to be cut off in the midst of my whining and worry and fear. Mel didn't need to hear that stuff, and I needed to be stopped from making my negative confessions.

So now Mel and I will do this to each other. Whenever one of us gets anxious or begins to talk negatively, we'll do the static routine, "Breaking up...breaking up..."

In order to guard what's coming into your life, you just might need to hang up on someone if the conversation gets too negative. In fact, you don't even need to pick up the phone if you know it's going to be a negative call. That's what voice mail is for, right?

Instead of words of negativity, we need to speak words of life to people. Here's what the Bible says in Proverbs 10:11: "The mouth of the righteous is a well of life."

Are you a believer in Jesus? Then He has made you righteous. So, according to this verse, you have words of life to speak to other people.

Here are five points to remember about the words that come forth out of our mouths:

Do it

Speak life to others. Speak life over yourself.

> The tongue of the wise promotes health.
> —PROVERBS 12:18

> A man has joy by the answer of his mouth.
> —PROVERBS 15:23

> Pleasant words are like a honeycomb, sweetness to the soul and health to the bones.
> —PROVERBS 16:24

> Death and life are in the power of the tongue, and those who love it will eat its fruit.
> —PROVERBS 18:21

Charles Capps, in his book *God's Creative Power Will Work for You*, said that God told him, "My word is not void of power. My people are void of speech....By observing circumstances they have lost sight of my Word....No word of mine is void of power, only powerless when it is unspoken. I have told my people they can have what they say, and they are saying what they have."[1]

Don't do it

Don't speak death to others. Don't speak death over your own life.

> He who guards his mouth preserves his life, but he who opens wide his lips shall have destruction.
> —PROVERBS 13:3

> A wholesome tongue is a tree of life, but perverseness in it breaks the spirit.
> —PROVERBS 15:4

> Whoever guards his mouth and tongue keeps his soul from troubles.
> —PROVERBS 21:23

The Boneless Tongue

The boneless tongue, so small and weak,
Can crush and kill, declares the Greek.
The tongue destroys a greater horde,
The Turk asserts, than does the sword.
The Persian proverb wisely saith,
A lengthy tongue—and early death!
Or sometimes takes this form instead,
Don't let your tongue cut off your head.
The tongue can speak a word whose speed,
Say the Chinese, outstrips the steed.
The Arab sages said in part,
The tongue's great storehouse is the heart.
From Hebrew was the maxim sprung,
The feet should slip, but ne'er the tongue.
The sacred writer crowns the whole,
Who keeps the tongue doth keep his soul.
—AUTHOR UNKNOWN

Here's another proverb about the tongue: "Don't talk so much. You keep putting your foot in your mouth. Be sensible and turn off the flow!" (Prov. 10:19, TLB).

There's power in doing it

If you want to change your life, you have to change your confession. Mark 11:23 tells us, "For assuredly I say to you, whoever says to this mountain, 'Be removed and be cast into the sea,' and does not doubt in his heart, but believes that those things he says will be done, he will have whatever he says."

Don't get your dos and don'ts mixed up

Don't be like a parrot that repeats everything it hears. Don't say what God says in one breath and in the next breath say what the devil says. Choose whose voice you will repeat.

And don't dig up in doubt what you plant in faith. James 1:6–8 says, "But let him ask in faith, with no doubting, for he who doubts is like a wave of the sea driven and tossed by the wind. For let not that man suppose that he will receive anything from the Lord; he is a double-minded man, unstable in all his ways."

Do what the greatest of doers did

Imitate God. Talk like Him. Speak His Word to others and to yourself. The number one thing the devil is afraid of is when you speak the Word of God. He knows he'll be defeated every time!

When people, even well-meaning people, speak negatively into your situation or hurl your way words of hurt, insult, discouragement, and, yes, even sympathy, think and speak things that are true, just, lovely, and of good report (Phil. 4:8), and close the door to negativity.

In closing this chapter, please understand that there is a difference between sympathy and God's compassion. Sympathy ends at "I feel sorry for you." God's compassion moves past empathy and can take His Word and put it into action to help see you through to victory. Let's have God's loving compassion for one another.

9

EXPECT SUPERNATURAL, MIRACULOUS POWER

OUR GOD IS a God of miracles, signs, and wonders. He will move heaven and earth to meet your needs—He loves you that much!

Do you know that Jesus' miracle ministry is still in operation on Planet Earth today? Jesus is the same yesterday, today, and forever (Heb. 13:8). Whether you need physical healing, emotional healing, healing for a broken heart, or deliverance from an addiction, Jesus Christ is alive and well and wants to bring you your divine breakthrough.

How do I know? Jesus miraculously healed me of second- and third-degree burns in just ten days, and He can heal you too! In fact, in Jesus' name, I set my faith in agreement for your healing this very day!

God loves you so much. And He delights to show up in your life and to show off—often in miraculous ways.

While my entire healing was a miracle in itself, let me share something special that He did for me while I was still in the hospital praying for my miracle. Remember, from day one, my face was wrapped in bandages. Daily the nurses would come in to take my bandages off, clean my wounds, and then re-bandage my face. The problem was, however, that as my raw face was healing, the new skin that was starting to grow back was sticking to the bandages. So when the nurses removed my bandages, part of my new skin came off too. Burn victims will relate to this excruciating pain. Now, since I was not on any type of painkiller, this daily process could not keep the tears from streaming down my face as much as I tried not to show any emotions on the outside, my inside screamed out to my Lord to help me get through the pain; and He did.

By day four of my hospital stay a lot of healing had taken place already, and I was able to stand up and walk. So on that day I walked to the shower. All the way I kept thinking about the bandages on my face having to come off, which, of course, I hated, because I knew that in the process the skin would come off too and I'd have to go through all that pain again. To this day I wonder about this concept: to put bandages on burn victims with no skin and then to have the new skin heal into the bandages. There has to be a better way to keep infection out!

On this particular day in the shower, when I started to pull off the bandages, which, of course, were stuck to my skin, I just started to cry. The pain was unbearable. I got down on my knees and began worshiping and praising God. Well, the presence of God filled that tiny shower room. I could feel the glory of the Lord being manifested. And when I opened my eyes and looked down on the shower floor, all of the bandages were lying there in a nice little heap. And I hadn't even felt them come off! Now that was a miracle, a supernatural intervention of God during my time of worshiping Him.

It was like the story of Paul and Silas in prison. They

began worshiping and praising God, and all of a sudden their chains fell off and an angel opened the prison doors and set the men free (Acts 16:25–26).

There's just something supernatural about praise and worship—and loving God—that invites His presence into your circumstance. He can take care of impossible situations in your life and in mine when we praise Him.

PROOF THAT HE'S A GOD OF MIRACLES

Just look at some of the ways God has shown Himself as God of the miraculous.

In the first chapter of Genesis we see that God spoke the world into being. That was the miracle of creation. When we watch the birth of a new baby, we are watching a miracle take place. It's a miracle that we can become born again and receive our salvation.

Perhaps Jesus being born on earth is the greatest miracle of all. Two thousand years ago God actually came down to earth with skin on in the person of Jesus Christ.

There's a story about a little boy calling out in the stillness of the night. "Daddy, I'm scared!" Dad responds by calling out to his son, "Honey, don't be afraid, Daddy's right across the hall." After a brief pause the little voice is heard again. "Daddy, daddy, I'm still afraid." This time Dad replies, "God is with you. He loves you." Finally the little boy calls out, "I don't care about God; I want someone with skin on!"

Possibly the logic used by this little boy is precisely the reason for the Incarnation. After thousands of years of unsuccessfully trying to convince His people that He really loved them, our Creator determined that the best way to demonstrate His love for us was to come down to us with skin on.

MIRACLE-WORKING BUSINESS

Jesus Christ was in the business of working miracles in the lives of those around Him. In essence, He had a miracle shop here on earth. When He returned to heaven, He left His miracle shop for Christians to run. It's something we've inherited, just as if a family member had a store, say a jewelry store, and left it for us to run. Jesus has left His miracle shop for us, and all we have to do is step into this shop for our miracle. Welcome to the family business of miracles!

You and I need to know how to run the business, so He left His instructions in His Word. In addition, we receive instruction through prayer. I like what Dr. Paul Yonggi Cho, who pastors the world's largest church in Seoul, South Korea, has to say: "The problem with the American church is that they pray for ten minutes and then preach for one hour. What they need to do is to pray for one hour and preach for ten minutes."[1]

I put a lot of stock in what Dr. Cho says, because he has the world's largest church and he's changed a nation. He took a war-torn country that was poverty stricken, and now he has many millionaires in his church, because he has taught them biblical principles for their finances and how to walk in faith to receive their miracles—financially and in every area of their lives.

Jesus made blind eyes see, lame people walk, and He raised people from the dead. His Word says in John 14:12, "Most assuredly, I say to you, he who believes in Me, the works that I do he will do also; and greater works than these he will do, because I go to My Father." This is Jesus talking to all believers—including you and me.

This is what's available to us if we want to carry on the miracle-working business that Jesus left behind, not only to receive our own miracles but also to pray for and see miracles happen in the lives of others.

In order to carry on the business of working miracles, there are certain things we must do. For example, in John 14:13–14, Jesus says, "Whatever you ask in My name, that I will do, that the Father might be glorified in the Son. If you ask anything in My name, I will do it." That sounds so easy, doesn't it? If I ask anything in Jesus' name, He will do it.

He says these are things that are available for you and me as believers, but then He goes on to give more instruction on how the miracle shop works. He says in verse 15, "If you love Me, keep My commandments." Then in verse 21, He says, "He who has My commandments and keeps them, it is he who loves Me. And he who loves Me will be loved by My Father, and I will love him and manifest Myself to him." Deuteronomy 4:1 tells us to keep God's commandments and live.

So He's telling us that we have to keep His commandments. Do you want the miracle shop to work right? Then keep His commandments. "Which commandments, Lord? The Ten Commandments?" Well, God makes it real clear in John 15: "This is My commandment, that you love one another as I have loved you. Greater love has no one than this, than to lay down one's life for his friends. You are My friends if you do whatever I command you" (vv. 12–14).

If Jesus is our friend, whatever He commands us to do, we do. So if we go into the miracle-working shop and want to run it the way Jesus ran it, He tells us what to do. Now I like the part that says if I ask anything in His name, He'll give it to me. But now Jesus is saying, "No, you give something to Me. You give Me your life by laying it down."

"But Lord, what about asking for anything in Your name?" So I make my list: I want this, that, and this. And He says, "OK, you can have all that, but first you come over here, and I'll show you how to get it. You give it all to Me." And then He'll tell you to do things that look like they're not lining up with what you're believing for. He may even say to give that thing away, or go here and do this or do that. And you begin to wonder just what the game plan is, anyway.

Do you want miracles, signs, and wonders in your life? Then in a way it will cost you your life. But most of us get into situations where we're about to lose our lives anyway. I sure did on that movie set that day. We get ourselves into places where we need miracles, signs, and wonders to survive. So we might just as well decide, "God, whatever You want with my life, I'll do it Your way." That way you stay living in line for divine health, and you stay in the path of blessings.

I don't know why it takes some of us so long to get this revelation or why we have to learn the hard way that it just doesn't work trying to live life our own way. The ways of the world bring sin, disease, death, and destruction. The ways of the Lord bring health, healing, prosperity, and blessings.

THE TWO GREATEST COMMANDMENTS

Jesus tells us in Matthew 22:37–40, "'You shall love the LORD your God with all your heart, with your soul, and with all your mind.' This is the first and great commandment. And the second is like it: 'You shall love your neighbor as yourself.' On these two commandments hang all the Laws and the Prophets."

This means we don't even have to worry about the Ten Commandments. We just need to be concerned about what Jesus tells us here. If we observe these two commandments, we'll be automatically observing the Ten Commandments.

HOW TO GET YOUR MIRACLES

How badly do you want your miracle? What kind of price are you willing to pay? Will you give up everything to get that miracle? Will you do whatever He says? If so, you will get your miracle; it's 100 percent guaranteed. But you need to do your part.

Point One is to develop intimacy with God, which is the beginning of the first and great commandment Jesus speaks of. It's loving and having an intimate relationship with Him. There are miracles, signs, and wonders in Him; intimacy with Him brings these things into our lives.

From time to time our church will fast and pray, where we give things up for a certain period of time to spend more time with the Lord. And it's very refreshing to the mind to have extra time to pray and spend time in the Word. There's nothing better than taking one week out of your life and cutting out every phone call, every communication with others, everything but Jesus. It's the most awesome thing to press into God in this way.

During my ten-day hospital stay, while lying in that bed, I could have turned on the TV, I could have chatted with friends, and I could have talked on the phone or read magazines. But I was in desperate need of a miracle. I didn't want to watch TV, I didn't want to talk to anybody, and right then I didn't want anybody to see what I looked like.

I was believing God for a miracle. I couldn't afford to look at my circumstances in the natural. Whatever is going on in your life, are you willing to pay the price to look at it in the supernatural? Of course, the natural is screaming for your attention. It screamed at me with words like, "You're scarred. You'll never have your face in front of anybody again, because you're going to be so embarrassed with what you look like. Your husband's going to want to get rid of you. He didn't plan to marry a woman without a face."

It's times like these when we need to shut everything else out and have nothing but Jesus and the Word. I had my whole mind and body drenched by the Word and literally would not think of anything but Jesus. I only wanted to be in His company and hear His comforting words. That's what happens when you spend time with Him and develop an intimacy that can only come when you choose Him over everything else.

You may be thinking, "Desiree, are you saying to cut everything out but Jesus?" Yes, if that's what it takes to get your miracle. Find the time, whether it's a day or two days. However long it's going to take to get your miracle, do it. Get alone with Jesus. Get to where you're only listening for His voice. The most awesome thing in the world for a Christian is the fact that you don't have to run to another person for counsel. You already have the Holy Spirit, the best counselor in the world, living inside you, and He'll give you divine guidance when you need it.

Increase the time you spend in prayer and in His Word. You may say, "I don't have enough time as it is." Then change. Do you want your miracle? Or do you want things to stay as they are? If you want your circumstances to change, you need to change. One of our favorite sayings should be, "Change me, Lord."

John 15:1–2 says, "I am the true vine, and My Father is the vinedresser. Every branch in Me that does not bear fruit He takes away; and every branch that bears fruit He prunes, that it may bear more fruit." Jesus is repeatedly pruning every branch that continues to bear fruit. Likewise, to make us bear richer and more excellent fruit, He keeps changing us.

Verses 3–5 say, "You are cleansed and pruned already, because of the word which I have given you [the teachings I have discussed with you.] Dwell in Me, and I will dwell in you. [Live in Me, and I will live in you.] Just as no branch can bear fruit of itself without abiding in (being vitally united to) the vine, neither can you bear fruit unless you abide in Me. I am the Vine; you are the branches. Whoever lives in Me and I in him bears much (abundant) fruit. However, apart from Me [cut off from vital union with Me] you can do nothing" (AMP). In essence, this is saying that apart from Jesus, you're not hooked up to get your miracle.

So again, Point One is that you need to have an intimate relationship with Jesus. You have to spend time with Him to get your miracle, be it a day, two days, a week, or more. And you just may have to do something to change yourself.

Point Two is loving other people. In the second command given by Jesus, He says, "You shall love your neighbor as yourself. On these two commandments hang all the Law and the Prophets" (Matt. 22:40).

Jesus is telling us to be loving and forgiving people. Not only can unforgiveness block your miracle, but it can also make you sick. I know how it is with me when I am going through an emotional trial, I usually get sick. If I'm under heavy persecution or spiritual attack and I am not responding or thinking with the love of Christ, all of a sudden, my immune system gets run down and cold symptoms, or other symptoms, try to come on me. I see the same type of thing happening to others in the church.

Emotions do affect us. Our relationships with other people affect us. In many of the cancer cases I've seen, there has been unforgiveness in the person's life. Often I've been able to zero in on the unforgiveness through prayer and fasting and listening to the words that come out of the individual's mouth.

I've discovered that as long as we live here on Planet Earth, every time we meet another human being, there is a potential to get hurt and offended. In fact, at one point following my healing, I had symptoms try to come back on me. I could feel the skin on my face tightening, and blister marks started to appear. Then God started to deal with me about keeping a loving and forgiving heart. As I forgave, healing manifested immediately.

GOD'S POWER AT WORK

I absolutely love watching God's miraculous power at work. I can remember once when my mom had a huge tumor on her knee. I prayed and laid hands on it, and it dissolved in my hands! Another time, Mom had a tumor in her cheek. Doctors had plans to operate on her, but they said that she would have a 40 percent chance of losing the ability to move the muscles on half of her face. Mel and I laid hands on her cheek, and the tumor dissolved. It was completely gone the next day.

Once we had a man in our church with a tumor popping out of his head. It was so bad and ugly that my first thought was that we'd need to organize a fund-raiser to help him out financially so he could go to the doctor. I have to admit that I was getting ready to pass out when I saw this bloody lump the size of an egg protruding from his head, but others had faith for this one. A group of us got together and prayed and believed for a miracle for this man. He came back the next day, and the tumor was off his head. One day it was popping out of his head. The next day it was gone!

Over the years, as we have prayed for others, Mel and I have heard more testimonies of cancers being healed. In fact, we've heard of every type of disease coming under the healing power of God. And I had so many supernatural experiences during my ten days in the hospital. I know Mel's favorite is when my bandages fell to the floor that day in the shower.

Remember my day in the shower? How could those bandages have just fallen off? Because God is a God of the miraculous. And just as He worked in my life, He wants to show Himself strong in your life too, no matter what you're going through. But you need to expect that He can do that for you.

Learn to expect supernatural things to happen in your life. Then sit back and watch the Lord work on your behalf in ways you couldn't dream of.

Second Corinthians 5:17 says, "If anyone is in Christ, he is a new creation; old things have passed away; behold, all things have become new."

Give God room in your life to do new things. I didn't want my old skin, the charred, second-and third-degree-burned skin. I stood on God's Word for my miracle and said, "No, I need new skin to grow." And that's just what happened.

What do you need new in your life? I needed new skin on my face. God gave it to me. Do you need a pain-free body, emotional healing, salvation, the gift of speaking in new tongues? Do you need a new house, car, or job? These are all miracles that our amazing, miracle-working God wants to give you. Allow the Holy Spirit to move in new ways in your life. God's mercies are new every morning (Lam. 3:22–23). Let Him work in you in ways you've never imagined.

Expect supernatural, miraculous power in your life!

Here is a prayer of faith for your miracle. Please pray it aloud:

> *Dear Father, I thank You that You created me. You are a God of miracles, signs, and wonders, and all things are possible with You. I am with You and not alone. I thank You that I am healed in every area of my life: spirit, soul, and body. I command pain to leave my body now, in Jesus' name. I command my body to be whole and healed as God*

created it to be! Sickness, disease, and affliction, you go from my life in the name of Jesus. I forgive everyone who has ever hurt me; I let hurt go in Jesus' name. Father, You created me whole and healed, and I will live my life in divine health all the days of my life. I love You, Father, and I choose to love everyone. Forgive me for every sin that I have ever done. I choose to live my life for You, and by Your stripes I am healed, in Jesus' name! I have a merry heart that does good like a medicine! I listen to good news that nourishes my bones! Your Word is health and healing to all my flesh, and I choose to meditate on it day and night! Your Spirit is alive inside of me quickening and healing my body! Thank You for my miracle! Thank You, Jesus!

10

EXPECT HEALING
IN ALL AREAS

W HILE I WAS still single and living in Manhattan Beach in the 1980s, and before I became a Christian, I was living a life of sex, drugs, and rock 'n' roll. In that lifestyle I contracted diseases as a result of having sex outside of marriage. One of the life-threatening diseases I had was syphilis, which gets into your bloodstream and never leaves. Once you get it, you have it forever. I had been given two documented reports by doctors, so I knew I had it.

Now, this is not something you really want to share with people. It's not anything I really want people to know about me. I believe as Christians we need to be more transparent and honest with one another. I know some of you reading this book have things in your life that need to be healed, and you need to know that the blood of Jesus can heal everything. God wants to heal you even though you might have been in sin and lived a wrong lifestyle, as I did.

I knew that when Jesus healed me of my burns from the accident, He healed me 100 percent of all my diseases. Because I had saturated myself in Him there in my hospital room and knew that the healing power of God was so strong in me, I got tested for syphilis when I got out of the hospital. It was gone! I've been tested twice since I was released from the hospital. Zero! No syphilis!

How is that? I believe I received my complete healing because I had ten days of nothing but God, with the Word going 24/7. I was so saturated in prayer and praise and the Bible, there were times when I could feel the presence of God so strong.

Expect God to heal you 100 percent. God wants you healed. He tells us in 3 John 2, "Beloved, I pray that you may prosper in all things and be in health, just as your soul prospers."

Here are other ways God has healed me:

- He replaced my compulsive eating with good eating habits and a healthy body.

- He replaced my compulsive lying with His truth.

- He replaced my fear with His love.

- He replaced my nightmares with dreams and visions.

- He replaced oppression and depression that I felt with His peace and joy.

- He replaced my low self-esteem with His boldness.

- He replaced my doubt and unbelief with faith.

- He changed me from being a gossiper and slanderer to a person of truth and edification.

- He changed me from being a people pleaser and compromiser to being a sold-out God pleaser.

- He replaced my hurt and offenses with a forgiving heart.

- When I was lost, He found me and saved me.

- When I was lying in the hospital for ten days with second- and third-degree burns, He gave me new skin for charred skin and left me with no scars.

- He healed me 100 percent from anorexia and bulimia. If that's an area you struggle with, you'll want to read my book God Hunger.[1]

If God did all that for me, think what He will do for you! Anything you ask. He loves you and wants to heal you in every area of your life!

John 10:10 tells us, "The thief comes only in order to steal and kill and destroy. I came that they may have and enjoy life, and have it in abundance (to the full, till it overflows)" (AMP). That's the kind of 100 percent healing Jesus has for you and me!

I have found in many years of ministry that much of sickness and disease is a lack of healing that really needs to take place in our hearts and minds. Most of us at one time or another have suffered from a broken heart. Now, the physical heart is also a big deal to the body. Take out your appendix, no problem. Take out your gallbladder, no problem. But take out your heart, and you're dead.

A granddaughter overheard conversations about her grandmother's occasional heart problem—loud beating, which made it hard for Grandma to sleep. One evening the little girl's father heard her concerned prayer: "And, Lord Jesus, please make Grandma's heart stop so she can get some rest."

Well, we don't want our hearts to stop, but I'm sure that many of us could ask for our hearts to be healed in the area of brokenness—and maybe even in the areas of hurt and offenses that have turned into bitterness that, when present, can bring pain and disease to our bodies.

HEALER OF BROKEN HEARTS

Jesus is the healer of broken hearts. Psalm 34:18 says, "The LORD is near to those who have a broken heart." Psalm 147:3 tells us, "He heals the brokenhearted and binds up their wounds." I have actually felt Jesus touch my heart when it has been hurt and bruised.

Our hearts are important. They are the center and the core of who we are. You and I need to take good care of our hearts.

How to have a healthy heart

Protect your heart

> Keep your heart with all diligence, for out of it spring the issues of life.
> —PROVERBS 4:23

Have a clean heart

> Create in me a clean heart, O God, and renew a
> steadfast spirit within me.
>
> —Psalm 51:10

> A sound heart is life to the body.
>
> —Proverbs 14:30

Magnify the Lord with your heart

> Be of good courage, and He shall strengthen your
> heart, all you who hope in the Lord.
>
> —Psalm 31:24

> Be glad in the Lord and rejoice, you righteous;
> and shout for joy, all you upright in heart!
>
> —Psalm 32:11

> I will praise the Lord with my whole heart, in the
> assembly of the upright and in the congregation.
>
> —Psalm 111:1

> You shall love the Lord your God with all your
> heart, with all your soul, and with all your mind.
>
> —Matthew 22:37

Have a merry heart

> A merry heart does good, like medicine.
>
> —Proverbs 17:22

A medical study, in which 122 men suffered their first
heart attack, evaluated their degree of hopefulness and
pessimism. Of the 25 most pessimistic men, 21 died
eight years later. Of the 25 most optimistic, only 6 died.
Loss of hope increased the odds of death more than 300

percent! It predicted death more accurately than any medical risk factor, including blood pressure, amount of damage to the heart, or cholesterol level.[2]

OUR MINDS

Focusing on disappointments, troubles, and overloaded schedules are mind problems and can lead to unhealthy minds and bodies.

Romans 8:6–7 tells us, "For to be carnally minded is death, but to be spiritually minded is life and peace. Because the carnal mind is enmity against God; for it is not subject to the law of God, nor indeed can be."

Remember, most battles take place in the mind.

How to have a healthy mind

Renew your mind

> And do not be conformed to this world, but be transformed by the renewing of your mind, that you may prove what is that good and acceptable and perfect will of God.
>
> —ROMANS 12:2

Here's how the Amplified Bible says it: "Do not be conformed to this world (this age), [fashioned after and adapted to its external, superficial customs], but be transformed (changed) by the [entire] renewal of your mind [by its new ideals and its new attitude], so that you may prove [for yourselves] what is the good and acceptable and perfect will of God, even the thing which is good and acceptable and perfect [in His sight for you]."

Think godly thoughts

Learn to magnify God more than the problem. In fact, magnify God more than anything!

> Finally, brethren, whatever things are true, whatever things are noble, whatever things are just, whatever things are pure, whatever things are lovely, whatever things are of good report, if there is any virtue and if there is anything praiseworthy—meditate on these things.
>
> —PHILIPPIANS 4:8

> You will keep him in perfect peace, whose mind is stayed on You.
>
> —ISAIAH 26:3

Cast down ungodly thoughts

> Casting down arguments and every high thing that exalts itself against the knowledge of God, bringing every thought into captivity to the obedience of Christ.
>
> —2 CORINTHIANS 10:5

Expect God's complete healing in your life.

DO YOU NEED FINANCIAL HEALING?

Mel and I had some trying financial times in our early days together. We were young, on fire for God, and excited about giving everything to Him—and we did. We gave away our car, clothes, and belongings. We enjoyed blessing others. Before long we were $30,000 in debt on a business project.

As we prayed and sought God's wisdom for our finances, He ministered to us through Dr. John

Avanzini's book *War on Debt: Breaking the Power of Debt*.[3] We began to apply both the biblical and practical principals we learned from our reading and study, and within one year we were completely debt free! God wants to do the same for you. Get wisdom, apply it, and see the results.

Three keys to help set you free from debt

Speak the Word, pray the Word, and confess the Word over your finances

Mel and I found scriptures that applied to us, wrote them out, and then spoke them daily. We put our written Bible verses in with our big pile of bills, and then we watched God move in a powerful way.

Give what you can

Luke 6:38 says, "Give, and it will be given unto you: good measure, pressed down, shaken together, and running over will be put into your bosom. For with the same measure that you use, it will be measured back to you."

Tithes and offerings

Malachi 3:10 states, "'Bring all the tithes into the storehouse, that there may be food in My house, and try me now in this,' says the Lord of hosts, 'If I will not open for you the windows of heaven and pour out for you such blessing that there will not be room enough to receive it.'"

One of my favorite scriptures is Ephesians 3:20: "Now to Him who is able to do exceedingly abundantly above all that we ask or think, according to the power that works in us."

Do You Need Emotional Healing?

Are you feeling stressed, oppressed, depressed, weak, and tired? Then you need God's peace and His joy.

Peace

> Rejoice in the Lord always. Again I will say, rejoice! Let your gentleness be known to all men. The Lord is at hand. Be anxious for nothing, but in everything by prayer and supplication, with thanksgiving, let your requests be made known to God; and the peace of God, which surpasses all understanding, will guard your hearts and minds through Christ Jesus.
>
> —Philippians 4:4–7

> The joy of the Lord is your strength.
>
> —Nehemiah 8:10

Do You Need Physical Healing?

Remember our passage from Proverbs, the one I stood on from the very beginning of my miracle healing process? It says, "My son, give attention to my words; incline your ear to my sayings. Do not let them depart from your eyes; keep them in the midst of your heart; for they are life to those who find them, and health to all their flesh" (Prov. 4:20–22).

"Health to all their flesh." All means all, complete, 100 percent healing from the Lord. That is His magnificent plan for you!

11

DON'T LOOK AT
THE NATURAL

B Y AROUND DAY five, my miracle had not totally manifested, but a lot of healing had already taken place. Still my lips were infected, and the whole area around my mouth was a mess, with pieces of dirt, gravel, and a white pus that was foaming with infection.

When the nurses came in that day to remove my bandages, one of them said, "Desiree, it's time for you to look in the mirror. You need to adjust to what you're going to look like." Now even though I hadn't seen my face yet, I knew that my upper lip was all corroded and infected. At the same time I had protrusions coming out of my wrists and on my face as well. They had to clean out the infected areas, which meant scrubbing on areas that were skinless. Ouch! The pain was unbearable, and many tears would roll down my face as I tried to endure the un-endurable pain. Up to this point I still hadn't looked into a mirror.

I knew to others I must have looked awful. Everyone who came to see me ended up crying. Mel, my strong man of God, my dad, and those who loved me. I knew things did not look good in the natural.

I can remember one evangelist who came in to pray for me who just walked right by my bed and asked, "Where is she?" When he saw me, he said, "Is that her?" All he could see were my eyes peering out of all the bandages and my bleeding, puffy lips. He couldn't hold back his gasp of horror as he recognized how badly I had been burned. He quickly walked out of the room to pull himself together.

I had to say no to the nurses when it came to looking at myself in the mirror. I wasn't going to identify with what I looked like at the time. I was going to identify with being healed. I hope you can get this. What things in your life are you identifying with? How do you see yourself? You have to see yourself healed before you're healed. That's faith!

The nurse wasn't happy with me. She thought I was just in denial. Well, she was right about that; I was in denial. I was denying the enemy the power to scar my face.

Throughout the room Mel had placed pictures of me from some of the shows I had recently worked on. He told me, "This is how you're going to look. In fact, you're going to look even better than this. God created you and He knows how to heal you, and He will!"

And so I said to the nurses, "I will not look in the mirror!" Even when I would go into the bathroom, I would turn my head so I wouldn't get a mental image of myself as a scarred burn victim. I chose to see myself whole and healed, just as God had created me to be. He made me, so surely He knew how to repair me.

Everyone close to me knew I was choosing to be in the Word of God 24/7 and was standing for my miracle.

I knew my God was not going to let me down. His Word is truth!

You know, when you're standing in faith for something, there will be people who will tell you that you're in denial and that you need to deal with reality. But I've learned not to accept what is in the natural, because I have an understanding of the supernatural that tells me that God, who is supernatural, can do anything on my behalf. The natural is subject to change. Jesus is the same yesterday, today, and forever. He healed people when He walked on Planet Earth two thousand years ago, and He still heals people today.

I've never seen more attacks on anything in the Christian body than the faith movement. Of course, the devil is going to stir up some grumpy unbelieving people to attack it. But who would want to come against someone believing God for a miracle? What's wrong with that? I've heard people say that someone they knew prayed for a miracle to live, but that person died anyway. Well, I have news for you; none of us are going to get out of here alive! But while we're living out our seventy or eighty years that we're promised, or however many years you are believing God for, I say let's get our miracles along the way!

Sometimes it's hard to take a stand when everything in the natural is contrary to what you're believing God for, but you need to guard your faith. The Bible says, "Faith is the substance of things hoped for, the evidence of things not seen" (Heb. 11:1). So for me, the substance of things hoped for and what was yet unseen was a complete healing.

Here are four keys for building faith for your miracle:

Believe

That's it? Just believe? Well, Jesus said in Mark 9:23, "If you can believe, all things are possible to him who believes."

This is from the story where a man brings his tormented son to Jesus' disciples, but they can't cast out the demon. So the man brings his son to Jesus for help.

Sometimes the natural circumstances seem like an impossibility to change. My burns were a good example of that. Perhaps you can name some of your own experiences where it seemed impossible for the circumstances to change. But don't believe what you see in the natural. Believe in the supernatural healing power of Jesus Christ.

Ask God to help your unbelief

It's only natural to have some unbelief. Look at the voices of doom and gloom all around you. But God will help your unbelief. I love the truthfulness of the man in the story above, which I believe opened the door for Jesus to perform the miracle in the man's son.

Mark 9:24 says, "Immediately the father of the child cried out and said with tears, 'Lord, I believe; help my unbelief!'"

In essence this man was saying, "Help me, God, as I look and see the son that I love being tormented by devils. Help me as I have cried a thousand tears wanting relief for my son. It's not for me, God, but for my son."

Perhaps you're asking God to help your unbelief in a certain area of your life. Maybe there's a mountain of bills that need to get paid. Maybe the doctors are saying that you have cancer, tumors, or some kind of disease. Ask the Lord to help you in your unbelief so that you can believe for a complete and total healing in whatever area you need.

Work on building your faith

Do you have a part in helping your unbelief? Yes, you work on building your faith. How? Remember what Romans 10:17 says. "So then faith comes by hearing, and hearing by the word of God."

Faith is like a muscle. You can build it. That's what I did in the hospital. I had nothing else to do as I was lying on that hospital bed, at times with no strength to move. So I listened to the Word of God, which not only built my faith but also allowed me to see myself healed based on God's Word. As I said earlier, you need to see your miracle before it happens.

Use the challenges and trials in your life to build your faith

Have you experienced any grief lately? If so, then that's an opportunity for you to build your faith.

Here's what the apostle Peter said: "In this you greatly rejoice, though now for a little while, if need be, you have been grieved by various trials [Did you catch various, which means many?], that the genuineness of your faith, being much more precious than gold that perishes, though it is tested by fire, may be found to praise, honor, and glory at the revelation of Jesus Christ" (1 Pet. 1:6–7).

Using our experiences of grieving and various trials allows us to know more about God and receive more revelation about His Son, Jesus. Trials make God-hungry people press into Him to a deeper level, where we receive more revelation, more wisdom, more understanding, and, yes, more faith! Faith is putting your complete heart trust in God.

Keys to Having Great Faith

Recognize the gift of creation

You are created in the image and likeness of God. Genesis 1:26 says, "Then God said, 'Let Us make man in Our image, according to Our likeness; let them have dominion over the fish of the sea, over the birds of the air, and over the cattle, over all the earth and over every creeping thing that creeps on the earth.'"

Ask God for visions and dreams

What do you see? What is the best thing that could possibly happen to you this year? And what if all things are possible, as the Bible says they are? Spend time alone with God and let Him give you His dreams and visions for your life…and ask Him to help your unbelief.

You have within you right now all the necessary elements to become all that the Father dreamed you would be in Christ. Ephesians 1:3 says, "Blessed be the God and Father of our Lord Jesus Christ, who has blessed us with every spiritual blessing in the heavenly places in Christ."

Be careful what you think about

Philippians 4:8 reminds us, "Finally, brethren, whatever things are true, whatever things are noble, whatever things are just, whatever things are pure, whatever things are lovely, whatever things are of good report, if there is any virtue and if there is anything praiseworthy—meditate on these things."

We have to watch what we meditate on and what we are thinking. We want to make sure we use the gift God gave us (our minds) to imagine the best in our situations, not the worst. Have you ever been driving in the car, or just sitting and thinking about an uncomfortable situation you have to deal with, and all of a sudden you imagine the worst that could happen? Make a decision to say no to these thoughts, and determine to replay that image in your mind, imagining the very best that could happen.

I had to do this for the year following my accident. I kept having dreams that I was on fire and that everyone else in my dreams was on fire. I would wake up in a cold sweat, feeling terrorized. One time while praying, I felt the Spirit of God telling me to imagine the dream over. I would go back in my mind and see myself quoting scriptures of life to myself and everyone, praying for the people in my dream, and watching the miraculous power of God healing them. Then I would pray for them as they asked Christ into their lives. I never had a nightmare after that, praise God!

Keep in mind that a polluted imagination will drain the life of God out of you.

Choose to meditate on God's Word

Joshua 1:8 says, "This Book of the Law shall not depart from your mouth, but you shall mediate on it day and night, that you may observe to do according to all that is written in it. For then you will make your way prosperous, and then you will have good success."

Now who wouldn't want to be prosperous and successful in life?

Read the Word

There's a reason why some Christians have power and some do not. And it's not because God is a respecter of persons, because He is not. Favor is a direct result of faith, and faith comes by obedience. When we pick up our Bibles, we must remember that this is a book with God in it; and His Word will breathe life into you!

Remember, Romans 10:17 says, "Faith comes by hearing, and hearing by the word of God."

Speak the Word

The purpose of all Scripture is to take us to this wonderful and blessed elevation of faith where our constant experience is the manifestation of God's life and power through us. Mark 11:22–24 says, "So Jesus answered and said to them, 'Have faith in God. For assuredly, I say to you, whoever says to this mountain, "Be removed and be cast into the sea," and does not doubt in his heart, but believes that those things he says will be done, he will have whatever he says. Therefore I say to you, whatever things you ask when you pray, believe that you receive them, and you will have them.'"

GUARD YOUR LIFE FROM THESE FIVE FAITH ROBBERS

Fear

Second Timothy 1:7 says, "For God has not given us a spirit of fear, but of power and of love and of a sound mind." If you have to confess this verse two hundred times a day, do so. As a stuntwoman I would find myself in some fearful situations. As I would continue to speak, "God has not given me a spirit of fear, but of power and of love and of a sound mind," faith would rise up on the inside of me.

Doubt

Don't doubt your faith. Instead doubt your doubts, which are totally unreliable.

Neglect of prayer and the Word

People do not have rich, beautiful faith when their spirits are denied the privilege of communion and fellowship with their Father. Make prayer and time in the Word your number one priority in life.

Draining relationships

If relationships in your life are not adding positively to your well-being, then they are taking away from you. While it's true that you might minister to everybody, in reality, it is wise to guard whom you allow into your intimate friendships. Our best example is that of Christ. He ministered to everyone, spent time with His twelve disciples, but only three people were in His inner circle.

I like what my husband says: "If God wants to bless you, He sends people. If the devil wants to curse you, he sends people." Make sure the people you are choosing as your best friends are sent by God. It's been said that you are like the five closest people to you. Make sure they are quality people that are helping you fulfill your God destiny!

Keeping your eyes on the natural

Finally, remember that you are in a war. The devil is fighting hard to make sure you keep your eyes on your natural circumstances, whether it be financial debt or sickness and disease.

I was in a war lying there in the hospital. While I was believing God for my miracle, the devil wanted me to focus on my accident and burned face, neck, and arms. I had to remember that my fight was spiritual. Ephesians 6:12 says, "For we do not wrestle against flesh and blood, but against principalities, against powers, against the rulers of the darkness of this age, against spiritual hosts of wickedness in the heavenly places."

I had to fight the good fight of faith and keep in mind that I was a soldier in the army of Christ. Second Timothy 2:3–4 says, "You therefore must endure hardship as a good soldier of Jesus Christ. No one engaged in warfare entangles himself with the affairs of this life, that he may please him who enlisted him as a soldier."

Recognize that you are in a war. Make sure to put on your spiritual armor every morning, and keep it on all day long. Ephesians 6:13–17 talks about our spiritual armor that will help protect us here on earth. It talks about truth, righteousness, and peace, which are so important for our protection. It talks about the shield of faith, which will quench all the fiery darts of the wicked. Isn't that an awesome promise? Every evil attack against you will fail as you hold up your shield of faith. And of course, there's the helmet of salvation, and finally the sword of the Spirit, which is the Word of God, our only offensive piece. Use it daily. Become skilled with your sword.

When Mel and I were in Israel in 1993, we noticed that even the young boys, some only fourteen years old, carried their weapons at their sides at all times. They even slept with them. How much more should we always keep our spiritual weapons at our sides?

Yes, you are in a spiritual battle, but know this: your Daddy God has given you every piece of weaponry you need to win your battle. He is on your side, and He will never leave you or forsake you. You are not alone in this battle. You will win if you don't give up!

12

EVANGELIZE AND SHARE THE LOVE OF JESUS

N O MATTER WHERE you are or what circumstance you find yourself in, there's always an
opportunity to evangelize. Even in my hospital
bed, while lying there with second- and third-degree
burns, I looked for ways to share my faith in Jesus. I was
able to share the gospel with a lady who was brought
into my room and placed in the bed next to mine. She
also had been burned. Lying in her bed, she accepted
Jesus as her Lord and Savior, and later she received the
baptism of the Holy Spirit.

There was a little boy down the hall who had one of
his arms fried off due to electrocution. When I went to
his room to share with him, he started telling me about
how an angel appeared and took him off the electrical
wire he was hanging on to. Before long we were doing
wheelchair races, praising God together and thanking
the Lord, while traveling up and down the hospital
hallways.

Shortly after my shower experience, where the power
of God was so strong that my bandages literally fell off
my face, I'd moonwalk down the hospital halls. Looking

like a mummy with my head still wrapped in bandages, I'd share the love of God with the nurses and just about anybody who would listen to me testify about my experience in the presence of the Lord.

I encourage you to look for opportunities to share the love of Christ, even in situations that otherwise might seem negative. See, what the devil meant for harm in my accident, God turned around for good and allowed me the opportunity to share His love in the Sherman Oaks Burn Center.

Winning a soul to Christ is the highest high you will ever experience as a Christian here on earth. It brings joy unspeakable when you lead someone out of darkness and into God's marvelous light.

Several years ago, when our son, Joshua, was ten years old, he flew out to meet Mel and me in Arizona. When I asked him how he liked his airplane flight, he told me how he led the lady in the seat next to him to the Lord and how he shared his Bible with her.

The Bible says that all the angels in heaven rejoice over one person making a decision to ask Jesus into their heart and choosing to spend eternity in heaven. So I encourage you, no matter your age, no matter what's going on around you, no matter what your circumstance is, keep that evangelistic spirit in you.

Here's what God's Word says about those who evangelize:

> Those who are wise shall shine like the brightness of the firmament, and those who turn many to righteousness like the stars forever and ever.
> —DANIEL 12:3

The fruit of the righteous is a tree of life, and he
who wins souls is wise.

—PROVERBS 11:30

EIGHT WAYS TO WIN SOULS FOR
THE KINGDOM OF GOD

Know your gift and use it

Whether your gift is hospitality and you bless your
neighbor, or whether your gift is giving and you finance
a missionary's trip, know your gift and use it to bring
souls to Christ.

What do you like to do? Then do it to win souls. Do
you like to go to the beach? Then take the gospel message with you. Do you like to teach? Consider a children's ministry at your church.

Find creative ways to use your gift to share the good
news of Jesus Christ.

Serve a soul-winner

As you associate with someone who has a heart to
lead others to Christ, you will learn how to effectively
share your faith. Whatever and whoever you are around
will have an effect on you. That's why the Bible says that
the righteous should choose his friends carefully (Prov.
12:26).

Follow Jesus

Jesus says in Matthew 4:19, "Follow Me, and I will
make you fishers of men." As we follow after Christ, He
will give us opportunities to share His love with others.

Get involved with a Bible-believing church

Make a commitment to your local body of believers.
You need the fellowship, and the fellowship needs you.

Psalm 92:13 says, "Those who are planted in the house of the Lord shall flourish in the courts of our God."

Church is a wonderful place to learn how to win souls. Make sure you fellowship where the gospel is preached and people are invited to receive Jesus into their hearts.

Pray

Your success or failure in winning people to the Lord is directly related to your prayer life. James 5:16 says, "The effective, fervent prayer of a righteous man avails much."

Pray in the Holy Spirit

We discussed praying in the Holy Ghost extensively in chapter 4. Praying in tongues gives you power. Acts 1:8 tells us, "But you shall receive power when the Holy Spirit has come upon you; and you shall be witnesses to Me in Jerusalem, and in all Judea and Samaria, and to the end of the earth."

Jude 1:20 says, "But you, beloved, building yourself up on your most holy faith, praying in the Holy Spirit."

Praying in tongues makes you sensitive to the Spirit of God.

Give

Meeting someone's need often opens the door to being able to share the gospel. People's hearts are touched when you reach out and do something good for them. The simplest act of asking someone if you can pray for them when they are not feeling well can open up a marvelous door for you to lead them to the Lord.

Ask God to give you a revelation of heaven and hell

Jesus said in Matthew 10:28, "And do not fear those who kill the body but cannot kill the soul. But rather fear Him who is able to destroy both soul and body in hell." And then He says in Mark 9:44, "Their worm does not die and the fire is not quenched."

The more we understand the reality of hell, the more we will risk stepping out in boldness to share our faith and testimony with others.

In heaven the streets are made of gold, and there are beautiful mansions for the children of God to inhabit. Let's make sure we are bringing others with us to this glorious place.

Here's one of the best verses of Scripture to help you lead someone away from hell and toward heaven where we will spend eternity with God:

> If you confess with your mouth the Lord Jesus and believe in your heart that God has raised Him from the dead, you will be saved. For with the heart one believes unto righteousness, and with the mouth confession is made unto salvation.
>
> —ROMANS 10:9–10

We need to recognize that our lives are about getting as many people as we can into the kingdom of God. We can't say it enough: Earth is short and heaven is long! We're only here on Planet Earth for a short season. That's it! The real life is going to be when we're in heaven. That's the real world. We're going to spend eternity there.

So, we have a short time to do something significant for God. We get one shot at it. And every year that goes by we need to ask ourselves, How many people did we bring into the kingdom? How much did we obey the voice of God to impact our nation for Christ?

God Uses Ordinary People

How can an almighty God use someone like you and me? He loves to take the least likely people who will do anything for Him, and then show Himself strong on their behalf. We will do great things for God when that happens. Can we win a multitude of souls? Yes, even you and I can do that.

A trick of the enemy is to get us to look at ourselves in the natural. When we do and see the flaws each one of us has, we'll begin to question our own effectiveness. But listen, God is not looking at our outward appearance. He's looking for hearts who are faithful to Him and who want to work on His behalf. He's just waiting to show Himself so strong in our lives that we will actually do things that shock even us.

It's like Mel and me being senior pastors of a megachurch. Who would have thought? This was not in our game plan. We had plans to be actors in Hollywood and were moving along that path. We certainly weren't planning to pastor a church. Mel and I did not attend seminary school, and had no formal training when we first started as pastors. But God had a whole other plan for our lives. Once we got on fire for Jesus, then all we wanted to do was to win souls and preach the gospel of Christ.

Always be watching for how you can share the love of Jesus with others. In the hospital I was able to lead people to the Lord and then see them baptized in the Holy Ghost, and it was really fun. My time in the hospital turned into having some real joy. The enemy's plots and plans were ruined. He tried to destroy my life, at the very least scar my face. Instead, I was miraculously healed and saw people in the hospital saved for eternity. Praise God!

My ministry at Sherman Oaks Burn Center did not end with my miracle healing. My doctor, Richard Grossman, has invited me to talk to patients in the hospital anytime I like. So every year I go to the center and pray for burn victims. As a result many have given their hearts to the Lord, and all the glory goes to God!

If you are not sure if you are spending eternity in heaven, please pray this prayer with me:

> *Father God, I love You! I believe that You sent Jesus to earth and that He died on a cross and rose from the dead. Jesus, come into my heart and be my Lord and my Savior. Be my best friend...I will follow You. Forgive me of my sins, and I forgive those who have hurt me. I let it go and choose right now to press forward to the call of God You have for my life. Fill me with Your Holy Spirit and every gift You have for me in the mighty name of Jesus!*

If you prayed that prayer, please contact us by phone at 818-313-9393, online at www.DesireeAyres.com, www.IHPChurch.org, or via e-mail, desiree.ayres@gmail.com.

Please write to: Desiree Ayres, In His Presence Church, 21300 Califa Street, Woodland Hills, CA 91367.

Contact us on Facebook (http://www.facebook.com/PastorDesireeAyres), and Twitter Pastor Desiree Ayres (@desireeayres).

13

TESTIFY FROM A HEART OF THANKSGIVING

I AM SO THANKFUL for all that God has done in my life—not just following my accident on the movie set but over the years, His loving faithfulness poured out on myself and His people. I believe developing an attitude of gratitude is so important for getting and maintaining our healing, as well as for wanting to testify about God and all He has done in our lives.

In addition, having a heart of thanksgiving serves to drive out negativity such as self-pity, oppression, and depression. At all times, but especially during tough times, it's important to remember to be thankful. I encourage you to make a list right now of at least ten things for which you are thankful. Immediately this will bring a healthier outlook to your mind. I chose to have a healthy outlook during my hospital stay, and even now I strive to make it a daily lifestyle.

Luke 17:12–19 relates the story of where Jesus healed ten lepers. These lepers had shouted to Jesus for His mercy. He told them to go show themselves to the priests. And the Bible says that as they went, they were cleansed. Now one of them, when he saw that he was healed, returned to thank Jesus, falling at His feet in thanksgiving. And Jesus said to the man, "Arise, go your way. Your faith has made you well [whole]" (v. 19).

Healing to the ten lepers meant that their sores and spots were healed. Only one of the men came back and thanked Jesus for his healing, however. This man had a heart of thanksgiving. And the Bible says the man was made well, or whole. I believe that even the parts of his body that had been eaten away by leprosy grew back, and he was made 100 percent whole.

I'm sure you'll agree that life is not always easy. It throws us some curveballs now and then. While Jesus has done a lot for me over the years, that doesn't mean the attacks of the enemy have stopped and there aren't challenges in my life. Admittedly, sometimes the challenges overwhelm and frustrate me. But it's then that I choose to go back to the Lord with a thankful heart. I choose to fight the good fight of faith.

Rather than stress over my circumstances, I say, "Thank You, Father, for all You have done for me." Sometimes I start by thanking Him that I will spend eternity with Him. No matter what happens here on this earth, I get to spend time without end with God in heaven. And then I can go on from there and thank Him for my husband, who is such an awesome man of God.

We all have things we can thank God for, and when we do, it keeps us in a healthy state of mind and heart. The Bible tells us, "A merry heart does good, like medicine" (Prov. 17:22). I like the various translations of this verse so much that I have listed them for you below:

A happy heart is good medicine and a cheerful mind works healing.

—AMP

Being cheerful keeps you healthy.

—GNT

A cheerful heart does good like medicine, but a broken spirit makes one sick.

—TLB

A happy heart is a healing medicine.

—Smith-Goodspeed

A glad heart makes a healthy body.

—BBE

A glad heart helps and heals.

—Moffatt

A glad heart is excellent medicine; a spirit depressed wastes the bones away.

—JB

A cheerful heart makes a quick recovery.

—Knox

The best medicine is a cheerful heart.

—Fenton

A joyful heart worketh an excellent cure.

—Rotherham

In other words, joy heals, but sadness, oppression, and depression can make you sick.

When a trial or challenge comes into your life, it's

up to you to decide how you are going to respond. You see, it's not the situation that matters but rather your response to your situation! God tells you how to respond. He says to laugh, not cry; to have a merry heart; not a broken spirit.

Laugh at Your Circumstances

Now this is an interesting scripture from Job 5:22: "You shall laugh at destruction and famine."

A friend of mine shared this scripture with me when he heard that my Golden Retriever was sick and could possibly die. My friend started to laugh. I didn't think my dog being sick was funny at all! Then he explained this scripture to me: When you are laughing at your problem, you are laughing at the devil and the fact that he is powerless next to God. Laughing reminds Satan that he won't win in our situation, but Almighty God, whom we serve, will win.

This started to make sense to me, so I started to laugh. At first I had to make myself laugh. I even rolled on the ground in laughter. Now half of my laughter was fake, but I decided to fake it until it became real. I went back to the vet a few hours later to visit my dog, and he was completely healed. Glory to God! The Bible calls us a peculiar people. I'm sure our laughter and acts of faith would seem strange to most people. But I definitely was thankful to God for healing my dog.

When you have a thankful and joyful heart for all that God has done for you, it's much easier to laugh at those things in your life that have potential to destroy you and leave you in want. Is this some new doctrine? No, it's the Word of God that will save your life!

Remember, the devil comes to kill, steal, and destroy. He wants you mad, angry, and oppressed. God wants you happy, joyful, forgiving, and loving; and He wants you to have a heart of thanksgiving. When you do, you are positioned on heavenly ground where healing is available. But when we find ourselves outside of His presence, there's potential for heartache and pain. Remember what the psalmist said in Psalm 16:11: "In Your presence is fullness of joy."

How Do You Get Joy?

Enter into His presence

Besides Psalm 16:11, there are other portions of Scripture that speak about joy:

> He will yet fill your mouth with laughing and your lips with rejoicing.
>
> —Job 8:21

> And my soul shall be joyful in the Lord; it shall rejoice in His salvation.
>
> —Psalm 35:9

> Make a joyful shout to the Lord, all you lands! Serve the Lord with gladness; Come before His presence with singing.
>
> —Psalm 100:1–2

> The light of the eyes rejoices the heart, and a good report makes the bones healthy.
>
> —Proverbs 15:30

Develop a heart of thanksgiving, and praise God in the midst of your trials. Acts of praise still the avenger—Satan—the enemy of your soul.

Following my healing miracle, especially during the first two years, I would feel my skin tightening up and trying to scar. So I had to keep standing on the Word. I'd go out and testify about what God had done for me and about His healing power, and when I did, I could feel my face loosening up again.

Stay alert, and if you feel symptoms try to come back on your body, continue to stand on the truth that healed you in the first place. Decide that you're going to remember what Jesus has done for you, and the scripture that says by His stripes you are healed (1 Pet. 2:24). You need to guard the word of your testimony.

> And they overcame him [the devil] by the blood of the Lamb and by the word of their testimony, and they did not love their lives to the death.
> —REVELATION 12:11

The following is what to do if you do not want joy and thankfulness in your life. Here's a somewhat humorous prescription for unhappiness:

- Make little things bother you. Don't just let them—make them!

- Lose your perspective of things, and keep it lost. Don't put first things first.

- Get yourself a good worry—one about which you cannot do anything but worry.

- Be a perfectionist. Condemn yourself and others for not achieving perfection.

- Be right, always right, perfectly right, all the time. Be the only one who is right, and be rigid about your rightness.

- Don't trust or believe people or accept them at anything but their worst and weakest. Be suspicious. Impute ulterior motives to them.

- Always compare yourself unfavorably to others, which is the guarantee of instant misery.

- Take personally, with a chip on your shoulder, everything that happens to you that you don't like.

- Don't give yourself wholeheartedly or enthusiastically to anyone or to anything.

- Criticize everything and everyone at church. Don't give big in the offerings. In fact, don't give at all.

Use this prescription for a while, and you will be guaranteed unhappiness.

How to Keep Your Joy

Read the following Scripture verses to know more about what the Bible says about joy:

A man has joy by the answer of his mouth.
—PROVERBS 15:23

The spirit of a man will sustain him in sickness,
but who can bear a broken spirit?
—PROVERBS 18:14

These things I have spoken to you, that My joy
may remain in you, and that your joy may be full.
—JOHN 15:11

I [the apostle Paul] am exceedingly joyful in all
our tribulation.
—2 CORINTHIANS 7:4

Count it all joy when you fall into various trials.
—JAMES 1:2

Here are some practical ways to keep a joyful and
thankful heart:

- Think about funny things.

- Remember God's benefits.

- Hang around people who lift you up, not
  those who bring you down.

- Daily make a choice to be thankful.

- Make a choice about what you will talk
  about.

- When you've been dumped on, laugh and
  tell someone something good.

- Talk the Word of God.

- Get back to the basics of your faith, and
  stay focused on Jesus and what He has
  done for you.

How to Lose Your Joy

A sure-fire way to lose your joy is to focus on your problems more than on the Word of God that contains your answers.

Many years ago a little boy was given a priceless possession: his deceased grandfather's gold pocket watch. How he treasured it! But one day, while playing around his father's ice plant, he lost the watch amid all the ice and sawdust. He searched and searched, becoming frantic, but he could not find his watch. Then he suddenly realized what to do. He stopped scurrying around and became very still. In the silence he heard the watch ticking.

God has given each of us a priceless gift of joy in Jesus. How easy it would be to lose our joy and thankfulness in the scurrying around of life. Yet it is always there to find if we will but pause and listen to the beautiful presence of Jesus in our hearts and remember all He's done on our behalf.

PART THREE

FROM STUNTS
TO SERMONS

14

GOD IS NOT A RESPECTER OF PERSONS

MY SPIRITUAL UPBRINGING, perhaps like many of you, was a bit bizarre. My father was a Christian Scientist, and I attended Christian Science Sunday school until I became a teenager. I attended Christian Science youth camp and even attended a Christian Science college in my sophomore year.

My mother grew up Catholic and got involved in the New Age movement following the death of one of my sisters, who died at age two when she fell out of the backseat of the car and hit her head on a railroad track. I believe that devastating experience caused my mom to search for comfort, meaning, and a purpose for her life.

She sought after God through a variety of cultic religions. I don't believe she intended to be involved in the occult, but I do believe that she was deceived and sidetracked by Satan while searching for the truth. My mom became a psychic. She would read people's minds and tell their fortunes using a deck of cards. I remember as I was growing up that she would always tell us what her

Christmas presents were before she even opened them, and she was always right.

My favorite toy growing up was the Ouija Board. When we'd play it, doors would open and shut, and objects would pick up and move around the house. I'd start to get fearful when this would happen, but Mom would tell me not to worry; that they were friends from her past lives just coming to visit. My mom is now a born-again and Spirit-filled believer, and has a true prophetic gift, not one perverted by the deceiver.

I remember, as a teenager, one day I went to answer the phone, and the receiver lifted up in midair and dropped to the floor. I started to run out of the house, but my curiosity sent me back to see who was on the phone. It turned out to be the lady from the health food store. Another time, when I came home, the stereo turned on by itself. This time I was so afraid I ran down the street to my favorite girlfriend's house.

My friend was a Mormon and we would sit on the hillsides for hours and talk about spiritual things. When we would disagree on something, she'd call me "Terry the Fairy, the Mad Scientist." (I went by the name Terry as a young girl. As I got older, I began using my middle name, Desiree, as my first name.) I'd call her "Annie the Fanny, the Moron Mormon," and we'd laugh and continue our spiritual talks, trying to convert one another to our own way of thinking.

MY SEARCH FOR TRUTH

I started to attend various Mormon meetings; Monday family night with my best friend and her family; Wednesday night "Mutual" at her church; and Friday night dances. I dated mostly Mormons at this time of my teenage life. Mormonism became one of many religions I would study as I was on my own spiritual search for truth.

When I was around fifteen, I started to attend psychic meetings where our main focus was getting people healed. We would channel energy, and the patients would feel better. The leader of the group wanted to groom me and paid quite a bit of attention to my abilities. I became quite proficient at mind reading and was introduced to astral projection, which is a process where you actually leave your body.

When I was sixteen, I moved to Florida with a girlfriend and lived in one of my grandmother's cottages on a waterway down the street from the ocean. There, I once again hooked up with group of psychics. Tables would lift in the air, and all kinds of weird stuff would go on when we got together.

One night I was lying on my bed trying to fall asleep when I had my first out-of-body experience. I simply went up to the ceiling of the room where I could look down and see my body still on the bed. I freaked out and somehow got back into my body. I ran to tell my girlfriend and my brother, who was staying with us at the time, what had happened. Later my brother gave me a book about astral projection and suggested that next time I decided to leave my body, I should go and visit Mom back in California. Brilliant idea. I remember thinking that I could visit my mom without paying the price of an airline ticket.

I know this is going to sound farfetched, but this really did happen. Whenever I tried to astral-project to visit my mom, I kept overshooting my spot in California and ended up in outer space. Listen, this is scary stuff. This is not something we want to be doing. But the devil had me totally deceived back then, and I just didn't know any better.

In outer space I would freak out and head back to my body. One time, which would be my last time trying these spiritual adventures, I had a difficult time getting back into my body. While I was in outer space, the most horrific, demon-like snakes and serpents, the size of skyscrapers, were everywhere. I couldn't get away from them as they lashed out trying to kill me. From my time going to the Christian Science church, I remembered the phrase "God is Love," which I chanted thousands of times, but I still could not get back into my body. Then I remembered the new age leader teaching us to focus on the "white light." I tried that too and said the words white light, but there was nothing but darkness; it did not work.

Now at this time I didn't believe in the devil, demons, or hell. That's how deceived I was. So what was going on? My world was being rocked. Now that I know what it says in the Bible about Satan transforming himself into an angel of light, I understand that the white light is nothing more than a disguise. I had been tricked, and I didn't know what to do.

Somehow I made it back into my body and then sat awake for the rest of the night, horrified by what I had seen. Now some of you might think that what I did and saw was induced by alcohol or drugs. But up to this point in my life I did not drink, nor had I tried any drugs. This was a genuine out-of-body experience.

I remember sitting on my bed that night telling God that until I was more spiritually advanced, I would not mess around with any of this stuff again. But I have to tell you, after that, I could feel myself shutting down to spiritual growth. It was just all too scary.

So I decided to consume myself with a life of fun. I wanted to be a normal teenager. I didn't want to know what my friends were thinking, and I purposed to shut down any spiritual giftings I had. I truly believe that the gifts we are given are from God. I believe that even before I became a Christian I had the gift of healing and prophecy and the gift of words of knowledge. But the devil tried to pollute these gifts for his glory with the outcome being death for myself and others. But praise God, I met Jesus, who showed me what the gifts are for and how to use them to glorify God. I purposed not to step out in any spiritual gifting until I had a couple of years of renewing my mind with the Word of God to make sure that everything I would see or say was backed up by Scripture. This is how to keep from becoming a "spooky spiritual Christian." Everything you do and say is backed up by God's Word.

MY BATTLE WITH COMPULSIVE EATING

Choosing to shut down my hunger to know God is what I believe led me to compulsive eating. I had a void inside of me that I was filling with food. During my sophomore year at college I went from 120 pounds to over 150 pounds. I couldn't fit into any of my clothes except my overalls, which I wore every day.

When I returned to California and began to pursue a career in the stunt business, I was too big to double for most of the thin actresses. I became obsessed with working out, losing weight, throwing up my food, and doing whatever was needed to take the weight off. I became an anorexic-bulimic. This was during the time when my stunt career was taking off. I looked great on the outside, but I was dying on the inside. I was desperate. That's about the time when God sent Mel into my life, and I became saved, baptized in the Holy Ghost, and married all within six weeks. (I need to add here that we do not recommend getting married within this short of a time frame. We recommend one year of dating and getting to know the person and getting premarital counseling.)

My spiritual quest for God was finally filled when I asked Jesus into my heart. Now my life was one of growing and learning, not spiritually searching.

When Jesus healed me of anorexia and bulimia, I became radical for Jesus. I knew He was real and had power to heal. I shared my faith with anyone who would listen. I worked out at health clubs and danced at studios. Through those two avenues I began sharing my faith with women battling anorexia and bulimia. I'd always bring my Bible to work with me on the various sets and read it out in the open. People would ask what I was reading, and I'd tell them. Daily, I was leading people to Jesus, praying for their healings, and seeing them baptized in the Holy Ghost.

HUMBLE BEGINNINGS

I became a Sunday school teacher at my church and was so humbled that God found me worthy enough to teach His Word to His children. What an honor! Teaching that Sunday school class is one of the highlights of my life. I was so proud to say to people on the movie sets that I was a Sunday school teacher. God took what was once a woman living a sinful lifestyle, not worthy in my own eyes to teach children, and made her a Sunday school teacher. If He can do that for me, He can truly transform anyone.

One day I decided to read a Bible study course book by E. W. Kenyon.[1] Mel, my dad, and some friends said they wanted to join me. Seven of us met on Monday nights to study the Bible together. After a few weeks one of my friends was diagnosed with a brain tumor. I asked if she'd come over to our house during one of our Monday night studies and allow us to pray for her. That night she was healed. We all praised God, and since we didn't have any musical instruments, we just pulled out our pots and pans and praised and prayed. My friend is now married to a man she met in one of my support groups for people with eating disorders and has children of her own. Glory to God! That was the beginning of our miracle ministry.

Word got out about our Monday night home Bible study group. People from all over began to attend, and God would show up and show off!

CHURCH OF OUR OWN

Mel and I became assistant pastors at the church we were attending, and a few years later we were sent off to start our own church. Originally we were to go to Florida to plant a church, but a year later we felt the Lord calling us to start In His Presence Church in the Los Angeles area. Our church is now eighteen years old and located in the Warner Center in Woodland Hills, Los Angeles. We have a beautiful forty-thousand-square-foot church with over three thousand wonderful people attending, and we're growing rapidly. We see many souls come into the kingdom weekly, and miracles are a regular occurrence. The presence of God is strong and a signature of our church. We have anointed praise and worship music with a variety of rock, gospel—you name it; we do it—and an eclectic fellowship. We love our church and what God is doing in and through His people. We have a weekly prayer meeting where over five hundred people come out at night just to pray!

Our amazing assistant pastors are now in Thailand, where they have a home and facility called Zoe Ministries to rescue at-risk children. We have sent another pastor out to take the dramatic arts to our city and the nation in a ministry called Eastern Sky Theatre Company. We also have our first church plant called New Life in His Presence Church near Magic Mountain. This amazing pastor was a former gang banger who received Jesus at our church, two miracle healings for his children, and a restored marriage. He served faithfully as our janitor, as an assistant to us, and in any and every area of ministry you can imagine. He was faithful with our ministry, and God gave him a debt-free church of his own!

We planted our second church in another part of Los Angeles. Another faithful partner is doing an amazing work in the Philippines that we support, which includes a mission's house, orphanage, crusades, and so forth. I had the privilege of doing one altar call there where I saw more than two thousand people come to Christ. Our church supports homeless ministries, prison ministries, and missions in Lebanon, India, and other places throughout the world. We recently launched a television ministry on the Church Channel, where we reach two-thirds of the world. Mel and I have had the privilege to travel all over the world and preach the gospel. God has done truly, exceedingly, and abundantly above all that we can imagine, think, or hope for. And we still feel like kids who are just on the brink of something huge; we are so full of faith and excitement for what our amazing God is going to do next!

God has that for you! He wants and desires to do exceedingly and abundantly above all that you can think or hope for. I believe the rest of your life will be the best of your life. I believe your best days are ahead of you. I am praying that your life is exceedingly abundantly above all you could imagine, think, or hope for. I pray this is the best year of your life and that you fulfill the God purpose that He has designed especially for you. God loves you!

Remember, God is not a respecter of persons. What He has done for me...He will do for you! Just look how far He's brought me—from the grips of Satan to His everlasting kingdom, from Hollywood movie sets to sharing the pulpit with the man of my dreams, from lying in a hospital bed with second- and third-degree burns and diseases contracted from my earlier life of sin to complete, 100 percent healing. If He can do all of that for me, He can do it for you. In fact, He wants to do it for you.

God has been so good to me, and I love to testify on His behalf and share the good news from the pulpit of our church, and now from platforms around the country, to anyone and everyone who is willing to hear. I love to share how God healed me from anorexia and bulimia, burns and diseases. But even more I love to share that Christ Jesus loves you more than you can imagine. He died for you and was raised from the dead for you. If you will but ask Him into your heart, He will enter in and give you eternal life with Him in heaven. He will fill you with His life and take you on the adventure of a lifetime. I can't guarantee that it will be an easy life, but I can assure you of this: He will be with you every step of the way. He'll never leave you or forsake you.

Every one of us, at some point in our life, will step out of this earth suit. Make sure you know that once you step out of yours, you'll step from this life into eternal life in heaven.

I invite you to write me and share your testimonies of healing and how this book has helped you.

NOTES

CHAPTER 1
BORN IN HOLLYWOOD

1. Desiree Ayres, *God Hunger* (Lake Mary, FL: Creation House, 2005).

CHAPTER 3
IN A CRISIS, CALL OUT TO YOUR CREATOR

1. "Capsized Man Phones for Help 3,500 Miles Away," Reuters, September 10, 2001. (See also http://www.biblecenter.com/illustrations/prayer.php.)

CHAPTER 8
CLOSE THE DOOR TO NEGATIVITY

1. Charles Capps, *God's Creative Power Will Work for You* (Tulsa, OK: Harrison House, 1976), 7–8.

CHAPTER 9
EXPECT SUPERNATURAL, MIRACULOUS POWER

1. Dr. Paul Yonggi Cho, *The Fourth Dimension* (Plainfield, NJ: Logos International, 1979).

CHAPTER 10
EXPECT HEALING IN ALL AREAS

1. Desiree Ayres, *God Hunger* (Lake Mary, FL: Creation House, 2005).
2. John Ortberg, *If You Want to Walk on Water, You've Got to Get Out of the Boat* (Grand Rapids: Zondervan, 2001), 159.
3. John Avanzini, *War on Debt: Breaking the Power of Debt* (n.p.: HIS Publishing, 1971).

CHAPTER 14
GOD IS NOT A RESPECTER OF PERSONS

1. E.W. Kenyon, *The Advanced Bible Course* (Lynnwood, WA: Kenyon Gospel Publishing Society, Inc., 1989).

PHOTOS FROM AUTHOR'S CAREER AND LIFE

Desiree's Stunt Composites

Desiree's Stunt Composites

Desiree working her first stunt job, doubling Lynda Day
George on the motion picture, *Cruise into Terror*

The stunt that went awry

MARCH: A shower for Liz, given by best friend, Ann Westmore (later Liz' maid of honor). Liz collected myriad presents.

Desiree's mom, Dorismae Kerns, with close friend Elizabeth Taylor

Desiree's mom, Dorismae Kerns, publicity writer at MGM Studios, receives a letter from close friend Elizabeth Taylor.

144

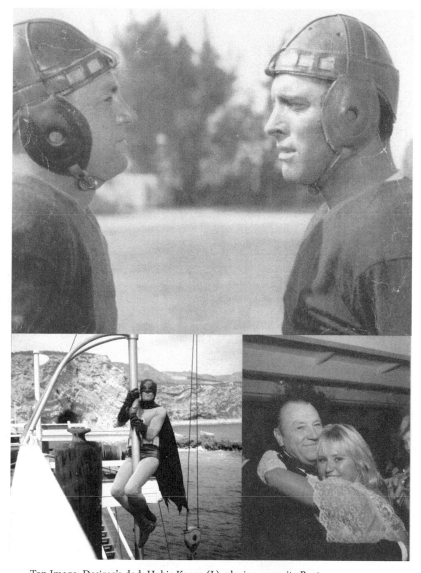

Top Image: Desiree's dad, Hubie Kerns (L), playing opposite Burt Lancaster (R) in the classic film, *Jim Thorpe- All American*

Bottom Left Image: Desiree's dad, Hubie Kerns, doubling Adam West on the his series, *Batman*

Bottom Right: Desiree and her dad at her wedding

Mel and Desiree Ayres today

ABOUT THE AUTHOR

DESIREE KERNS AYRES was born in Hollywood. Her dad was the stunt coordinator and stunt double for Adam West in the hit series, Batman. Her mom was a publicity writer for MGM studios and one of her clients, who became her close friend and the godmother of Desiree's brother, was Elizabeth Taylor. Desiree grew up in and around motion pictures and became a top working stuntwoman doubling Catherine Bach on the hit series Dukes of Hazzard, Heather Thomas on Fall Guy, working on Matt Houston, Knight Rider, and many others.

The last stunt Desiree did was dive out of a truck and the stunt went awry. She found herself at the Sherman Oaks Burn Center in critical condition in the Intensive Care Unit with second- and third-degree burns on her face, neck, chest, and arms, fighting for her life with her upper lip burnt off.

Desiree had been a born-again, Spirit-filled Christian for two years before this accident and knew the miracle working power of God. She was about to experience it for herself. In ten days she walked out of the hospital whole and healed thanks to Jesus Christ!

Desiree now co-pastors with her husband, Mel Ayres, In His Presence Church, a multicultural megachurch, where miracles happen on a regular basis. They launched a TV ministry reaching two-thirds of the world airing several times a week on various broadcasting stations.

They have sent out two churches in the Los Angeles area. They have sent pastors and missionaries to Thailand where they buy back at-risk children, and raise them. They have also built three churches in India. They have missionaries on the field in the Philippines where they have built a missions home, orphanages, and a Bible school. They also support works in Lebanon, and all over the world.

Desiree also travels and preaches, where her mission stays the same: populate heaven, plunder hell, and be a vessel for God to use to heal and encourage His people, while having some fun doing it!

CONTACT THE AUTHOR

PLEASE WRITE TO:
Desiree Ayres
In His Presence Church
21300 Califa Street
Woodland Hills, CA 91367

CONTACT US BY PHONE:
818-313-9393

E-MAIL:
desiree.ayres@gmail.com

VISIT OUR WEBSITES:
www.DesireeAyres.com
www.IHPChurch.org

FACEBOOK:
http://www.facebook.com/PastorDesireeAyres

TWITTER:
https://twitter.com/#!/desireeayres

Notes

Notes

Notes

Notes

Notes

Notes